SOME RECOLLECTIONS OF A BUSY LIFE

BY T.S. HAWKINS

The forgotten story of the real town of Hollister, California

REISSUED 102 YEARS AFTER ITS ORIGINAL PUBLICATION

WITH A NEW INTRODUCTION BY DAVE EGGERS

GREAT-GREAT GRANDSON OF T.S. HAWKINS

Copyright © 2015 T.S. Hawkins and Dave Eggers.

"An Actual Place Called Hollister" was originally published in the *New Yorker*.

Cover design by Jessica Hische.
Illustrations by Wesley Allsbrook.

Some Recollections of a Busy Life was originally published by T.S. Hawkins and printed by Paul Elder and Company of San Francisco, California, in 1913.

This edition was published in cooperation with McSweeney's Publishing of San Francisco, and printed by Thomson-Shore Printers in Dexter, Michigan.

978-1-940450-89-6

*For all the descendents of T.S. Hawkins,
and for the town of Hollister, California*

PREFACE

Some Recollections of a Busy Life, by T.S. Hawkins, was originally published in a very small edition—only three hundred copies—in 1913. Only a few books from this original printing remain.

In 2015, one of Hawkins's great-great grandsons wrote an essay about the book and the town of Hollister, and this essay is reprinted here to serve as an introduction to Hawkins's autobiography.

AN ACTUAL PLACE CALLED HOLLISTER

AN INTRODUCTION
BY DAVE EGGERS

Not long ago, I woke up one morning and thought it would be a good day to go to Hollister. I'd been seeing those hoodies around, and the place had been on my mind, so I found an old atlas in my garage, checked the map of California to make sure I remembered how to get there, and left. No one was expecting me and I wasn't expecting anything. It was the kind of trip a middle-aged man takes when his children are at a trampoline birthday party.

The drive took two hours from the San Francisco Bay Area, south on 280 to 85 to 101 to 25. Along 280, there are tens of thousands of acres of heavily wooded hills surrounding the Crystal Springs reservoir. It is incalculably valuable land, all of it protected. Eventually, it flattens out a bit, and the climate gets drier as you drop into the Central Coast. The hills go from green to gold, but are no less beautiful. Soon, there are farms on either side of the highway, and pumpkin sellers and stables and dust. It feels very Old West, and you're only an hour or so from San Francisco.

Hollister emerges in no particular hurry. Tidy rows of onions, cherry trees, and bell peppers give way to a small factory or two—a group of women in hairnets were taking a break in front of Marich Confectionery as I passed—and then there are diners and gas stations and, finally, a downtown that seems timeless without being in any way quaint. There is a beautiful red brick church, Hollister United Methodist, and, within walking distance, an array of well-kept Victorian homes, but there are empty storefronts and vacant offices, too. On the town's main thoroughfare, San Benito Street, I drove past an office building with a sign in the window:

**THIS BUILDING IS NOT EMPTY
IT IS FULL OF POTENTIAL**

Nearby, a pair of women were standing on a corner holding signs that said "Pray to End Abortion." Behind them was a pawnshop, and down the way Hazel's Thrift Shop and a motel called Cinderella— not to be confused with the nearby quinceañera and bridal shop, which offers clothing for "both novias and princesas." The town bleeds into agriculture on all sides, and beyond the farms are the hills, largely unmarred by any construction.

It is a strangely complete town, like something out of a Richard Scarry book. There are factories, farms, schools, railroads, horses, sheep, goats, and barns. There are men wearing cowboy hats and driving pickup trucks. There is a baseball card shop. A sign for the high-school homecoming dance advertises its theme: A Disney Ball.

I'd been to Hollister twice since I moved to the West Coast from Illinois, twenty-three years ago. Each time, I made a point of first visiting the old Hazel Hawkins Memorial Hospital. On this visit, I remembered it being close to the town center, and, sure enough, I found it easily. But something seemed different. A sign out front read "Prayer is the best way to get to Heaven—but trespassing is faster." Then, on the corner of Hawkins and Monterey, I saw a large sign that said "For Lease." This was new to me—what was once a town centerpiece, a delicate Spanish colonial with Italianate flourishes, had apparently been carved up into small offices. I parked and looked more closely.

I figured that given the building's origin as a hospital, and its status as one of the town's oldest buildings, the occupants would be of the nonprofit sort—Junior League, Historical Society, Ladies' Auxiliary. So I walked up the left-leaning white steps, noting that the sculpted cherubs on the front portico had been repainted without great care. To the right of the front door, a sign in the bay window announced, "FREE First Month Rent. Great Deals." Through the window, I could see a desk, and on it an early-nineties computer in the beginning stages of decomposition. The contrast between the building's rococo exterior and its garage-sale interior was startling.

In the lobby, on a low table, there was a tidy array of brochures and business cards for taxi operators, churches, faith healers, and purveyors of bail bonds. To the left was the New Light Embassy, which billed itself as a "Whole Brain Learning & Hypnotherapy Center . . . Enriching, Developing, and Empowering, the Human Potential." Occupying much of the right wing of the building was the NewLife Worship Center.

But there was no one inside. No one in the New Light Embassy, no one in the NewLife Worship Center. "Did you know Jesus attended church?" a green leaflet asked. "This is something we do not hear about often, but it is true." Then, in the sad silence of the dormant building, there was a sound. A thumping. I followed it down the hallway to a door. A floor mat in front said "Eli's Chop Shop," alongside a tricolored barber pole. Voices could be heard amid the hip-hop, and for a second I was so happy to know that there was someone in this building that I thought about going inside. But instead I left.

On the front lawn, under an old willow, I stood with no clear idea of what to do. I watched a man across the street cutting his grass and I cycled through a series of conclusions and emotions. I was saddened by the state of the building. The interior was gloomy, and the tenants seemed temporary and uncommitted to the upkeep of the building. And I cared about this why?

Fifteen years ago, the word "Hollister" meant little to anyone who didn't live in the town. Now it's hard to walk around any city, from Melbourne to Montreal to Mumbai, without seeing it stitched on someone's shirt or hoodie. Abercrombie & Fitch, which launched Hollister in 2000, has done an extraordinary job with brand penetration: in 2013, there were five hundred and eighty-seven Hollister stores around the world, and the brand netted more than two billion dollars in sales.

The clothes themselves rarely depart from the realm of sweatshirts and sweatpants—they're eerily similar to the comfort-wear you can buy at Target or Walmart. But a Hanes hoodie at Target is thirteen dollars, while a Hollister hoodie is $44.95. This implies that "Hollister" itself means something and is worth something.

For years, employees of Hollister stores, during orientation, were given the story, and it goes something like this: John M. Hollister was born at the end of the nineteenth century and spent his summers in Maine as a youth. He was an adventurous boy who loved to swim in the clear and cold waters there. He graduated from Yale in 1915 and, eschewing the cushy Manhattan life suggested for him, set sail for the Dutch East Indies, where he purchased a rubber plantation in 1917. He fell in love with a woman named Meta and bought a fifty-foot schooner. He and Meta sailed around the South Pacific, treasuring "the works of the artisans that lived there," and eventually settled in Los Angeles, in 1919. They had a child, John, Jr., and opened a shop in Laguna Beach that sold goods from the South Pacific—furniture, jewelry, linens, and artifacts. When John, Jr., came of age and took over the business, he included surf clothing and gear. (He was an exceptional surfer himself.) His surf shop, which bore his name, grew in popularity until it became a globally recognized brand. The Hollister story is one of "passion, youth and love of the sea," evoking "the harmony of romance, beauty, adventure."

None of this is true. Abercrombie & Fitch's brands—including the now-defunct Gilly Hicks and Ruehl No. 925—all have had fictional backstories, conceived by Mike Jeffries, the company's former C.E.O. Abercrombie & Fitch told the Los Angeles Times that the company pulled the name Hollister out of thin air, so any connection between the brand and the town is coincidental. Even so, the company's relationship with Hollister, California, population thirty-six thousand, has not exactly been one of benevolent indifference.

AN ACTUAL PLACE CALLED HOLLISTER

In 2006, a Hollister merchant put "Rag City Blues: Hollister" on vintage blue jeans and decided to file a federal trademark application for her label. She subsequently received threats from attorneys representing Abercrombie & Fitch. She was baffled; the lawyers had told her, in essence, that putting her town's name on the clothing would provoke a lawsuit—that the trademark attached to its brand superseded the rights of the town. (The company sees its legal opposition to the merchant as strictly a trademark issue, which has nothing to do with the merchant's being from Hollister.) According to the *L.A. Times*, students at a local high school worried that their sports uniforms would engender more legal letters. In an effort to smooth things over, town leaders suggested to Abercrombie that the company open an outlet in Hollister. It seemed to make sense—a Hollister store in the town of Hollister—but they were told that the company's aspirational brand would not find the right audience in Hollister. (The company does not have any recollection of this request.)

The town has no mall and few boutiques or cafés. It is not considered a tourist destination, like nearby Salinas, the home of John Steinbeck, or Gilroy, known as "the garlic capital of the world." Many of its older residents are Caucasian, but Hollister's demographics have been changing for the past fifty years, and today sixty-seven per cent of residents identify as Latino. Most of them work on the surrounding farms or in the few nearby factories. Hollister is an unglamorous town, but its name is now associated with some degree of taste and status all over the world. Which is odd, because the town benefits in almost no way from this success.

The rise of the Hollister brand has been especially strange to me, because it was my great-great-grandfather T. S. Hawkins who helped found the town of Hollister. Growing up, I was confronted daily by his white-bearded face, in an old photograph that hung in our living room in Illinois. A few feet away, his rifle, which he carried from Missouri to California, rested over our mantel.

The real story of Hollister begins in Marion County, Missouri, twenty miles from Mark Twain's home town of Hannibal, in 1836. This is when T. S. Hawkins was born, the eldest of nine children, his parents farmers, their people having travelled from Ireland and England and Scotland to the early Virginia settlements.

The Hawkins family lived in two adjoining log cabins with one roof covering both. The boys of the family slept in the attic, near the clapboard roof, and listened to the tapping of the rain in the summer. "The boards made a good roof to turn off the rain," Hawkins wrote in his autobiography, *Some Recollections of a Busy Life*, self-published in 1913.

> But in the winter when the wind blew the fine snow would drift through the interstices between the boards of the roof. It was glorious up in the old-fashioned feather bed, with the blankets pulled up to one's ears, listening to the roar of the wind, the pelting of the hail and snow and the war of the elements, until one fell asleep.
>
> In the morning, we would awake to find the bedding and the floor covered an inch or more in drifted snow. . . . It seems at this distance a rough life; but I do not remember that we ever considered it so, and it certainly served to make one hardy and self-reliant.

They hunted squirrels and quail and the occasional 'possum, and they ate their own pigs, in bacon and ham form, three times a day, for months on end. They made wool clothing for special occasions, but for everyday clothes they used bark—bark of "various trees," Hawkins notes, though it's hard to picture the clothing. You have to assume it was a fabric that breathed.

Hawkins attended the customary one-room schoolhouse, a few months a year, until he was sixteen. At that point, with his younger brothers able to take on his duties at the farm, Hawkins was freed to pursue his education. He made out for Kentucky, to live with his grandfather, a journey of five hundred miles, which for a "diffident, awkward, backwoods boy" felt "like going out of the world."

He tried his hand at teaching, and then medicine, before

returning home with three hundred dollars.

> I was content to remain idle for a short time, spending my days floating down the Meramec in my canoe or resting under the shade of the trees. But this could not last long, and soon I commenced to look around for something to do. From our home the nearest village was twenty miles. Scattered here and there was a country store. There was none nearer than seven or eight miles from our place, and I conceived the idea that I could establish myself in the business....
>
> I immediately went to work with a carpenter, and by the end of July, I had a building twenty by forty feet, with shelving and counter complete. I had already gone to St. Louis to a firm who were engaged in the business of furnishing country stores, and as I was entirely ignorant of what I needed, they selected a stock invoicing about two thousand dollars, on which I paid my three hundred dollars, and the balance they carried for me.

It's important to note several things at this point. First, a wholesaler provided T. S. Hawkins with two thousand dollars' worth of goods, which in today's currency would be about fifty thousand dollars. Second, although Hawkins had no experience in retail sales, the wholesaler was risking the credit, with no collateral. Third, Hawkins was all of twenty-one years old.

The store was successful. Hawkins served as his own "clerk, janitor, bookkeeper and everything else." When it got dark, he would go home for his evening meal before returning to the store, where he would "pull a cot from under the counter, make it up, and sleep until morning with a gun by my side. As a good many rough characters visited the mountains, it was not considered safe to leave the store, a half mile from the nearest house, over night."

The next year, he married Catherine Patton, a well-bred woman from two old Southern families. Within a year, her health began to fail, and their doctor recommended that they move to a milder, drier climate. Hawkins sold up, and began preparing for a trip out West. By the time he was ready, he and Catherine had a baby, a boy named T.W., and the travelling party had grown to twenty people, including Hawkins's father and his brother-in-law, along with sixty head of cattle, four wagons, fourteen horses, and seventeen oxen.

This was not the great emigration of the gold rush, ten years earlier. The Hawkinses saw other wagons only intermittently. They expected to come across ample bison to shoot and eat, but found none; during the journey, they were able to kill only two antelope.

Instead, they relied on trade with Indians, with other travellers, and with settlers. There had recently been a notorious event, the Mountain Meadows massacre, in southern Utah, in which a hundred and twenty men, women, and children from Arkansas were killed by Mormon militias masquerading as Native Americans, and so the Hawkins party joined forces with another wagon train heading West from Illinois. But the Mormons they encountered as they neared Salt Lake were friendly, Hawkins wrote.

> As we had been living on bacon and salt meats, with no vegetables for so long, I sought out a large house which I thought gave promise of affluence. I knocked on the front door, but received no answer, so I went to the back of the house, where under a tree sat a large, solid-looking man with a babe on each knee, while a dozen other children, from two to eight years, were playing around. Two women were washing clothes in the same tub, while a third was hanging them (the clothes, not the women) out to dry. It was my first view of polygamy. The man, as all others I met later, looked fat and happy, while all the women looked tired and careworn.

They travelled across the Bear River, and only then did they experience the kind of hardship and tragedy that all Western travellers had come to expect.

> In the Illinois company was a dare-devil of a young man, and when the cattle were well into the river he followed them on his horse. He had about reached the middle, the horse swimming gallantly, when the man and horse suddenly disappeared. After a time the horse came to the surface further across, but we never saw the young man again. We camped on the bank and all hands turned out to search for the body. The ferryman assured us that it was entirely useless, that Bear River never gave up its dead.

They traversed the Sierra Nevadas. They found Angels Camp and French Camp and crossed the Livermore Valley southwest to San Francisco Bay, near Milpitas. Hawkins finally arrived in Mountain View in 1860.

"So ended our journey across the plains," he wrote. "I have read somewhere the saying that the 'Good Lord takes care of children and fools.' Looking backward, I cannot but feel that we must have belonged to one or both of those divisions of humanity."

The health of Catherine Hawkins initially improved, but she died less than two years after the journey. To some, this would have seemed like a cruel trick played by a malevolent god. But Hawkins decided to stay in California.

> Only those who have lost the companion of their young manhood can know the utter darkness that can come and the feeling that the bottom has dropped out of one's hopes and aspirations, that the world has come to an end, so far as one's own life is concerned. I realized, however, that hard work and unceasing work was the only panacea for me.

Hawkins bought two hundred acres just north of Gilroy and married Emma Day, the daughter of a farmer. In 1864, they had their first child, Charles, and by 1867 Hawkins was a father of four and a prosperous farmer. Though he was largely self-taught, that year he shipped, he wrote, ten thousand centals of wheat to San Francisco.

Hawkins soon heard about a Colonel W. W. Hollister, who owned twenty- one thousand acres of agricultural land nearby. For many years, that land had been in the hands of Spanish clergy, after most of its Native American inhabitants had been expelled or drawn into the mission system. When Mexico gained independence from Spain, much of it was given to Mexican soldiers and settlers. After the Mexican- American War, Hollister bought his tract of land from Francisco Pérez Pacheco. Hollister had followed a southern path to California, from Ohio down through New Mexico and Arizona to Santa Barbara and then north. He'd started out with eight or nine thousand head of sheep, intending to move the largest herd of its kind across the continent. By the end, he had only a few thousand left, but when the Civil War began Hollister made a fortune selling wool that outfitted the Union Army.

By 1868, Hollister was ready to sell his property, part of a ranch known as San Justo. Hawkins organized a group of local farmers to buy the parcel for three hundred and seventy thousand dollars. They split the land into fifty tracts, leaving a hundred acres in the center for a town site. They were about to name the town San Justo when one of the men objected. Does every town in California have to be named after a saint? he asked. And so, after much debate, the farmers settled on

Hollister, honoring the character Hawkins called "one of the noblest men I ever knew."

Hawkins had one more child, and gave up farming to establish the Bank of Hollister. Eventually, his five children had eleven children among them, and all but one thrived. Hazel Hawkins, born in 1892, died at the age of nine, of appendicitis, although the illness isn't mentioned in *Some Recollections*. In the hundred and sixty-one pages of his memoir, Hawkins seems stoic, even cavalier, about any adversity or loss, but the death of Hazel Hawkins left him devastated.

"She had lived with us all her little life. She was my constant companion, and we loved each other with a devotion I had never known before. All of her days she had striven unselfishly to make all around her happy," Hawkins wrote. "On the fifth of March, as I stood by her bedside, she opened her eyes and looking at me said in her sweet voice, 'Goodnight, Grandpa,' and then fell asleep, to waken in the Paradise of God."

Hawkins blamed his granddaughter's death on the lack of proper health care in rural Hollister, so he threw himself into the construction of a solution and a monument. He named it the Hazel Hawkins Memorial Hospital.

I stood on its white stone steps, wondering what had happened. Looking for some insight into the state of the building, I went to Hollister's chamber of commerce. But first I had to wait. The chamber's president and C.E.O., Debbie Taylor, was occupied with a woman who wanted to know about the local Boy Scout troop. She was a new arrival, and a talkative one, having high expectations for the Scouts of Hollister. While I waited, I flipped through the brochures on a table in the office. "Wanted!" a flyer said. Apparently, the Hollister Hills Junior Off-Highway Rangers, a group of young A.T.V. riders, were looking for members to rampage through the surrounding golden hills.

When I got a chance to talk to Taylor, I asked about the golden hills, commending the city for preserving them. Taylor was not so sure she agreed. It might not have been the official chamber-of-commerce line, but Taylor implied that the town would not mind anyone building on the hills. They wouldn't mind economic development of any kind. The recession had been tough, Taylor said, and they were looking for any bright spots. There were too many tattoo parlors, she told me, and she lamented the karate studio that had recently closed under suspicious circumstances.

Without much prompting, we arrived at the subject of Abercrombie & Fitch, and Taylor talked about the litigation the company threatened and about the interesting fact that it refused to open a Hollister store in Hollister. But, she said, the town would soon have a Walgreens, and everyone was excited about that—no one more so than Debbie Taylor.

She asked me what brought me to Hollister, and I told her about T. S. Hawkins and my connection to him. She flipped through my copy of *Some Recollections,* and I showed her the photo of young Hazel Hawkins and explained the connection between her and the hospital in her name.

"Oh!" Taylor said. "You know there's a ribbon-cutting tonight at five-thirty?" I didn't know. I had no idea what she was talking about. She explained that a new wing of the relocated Hazel Hawkins hospital, a women's center, had just been built, and a few hours hence there would be an opening. She gave me the address—it was far from the site of the original building—and I left, the two of us marvelling at the lucky timing of my visit.

It seemed as good a reason as any to get a haircut.

I went back to the old Hazel Hawkins Memorial Hospital building and opened the door of Eli's Chop Shop to find a large tattooed man behind a barber's chair cutting the hair of another large tattooed man. In a second barber's chair, there was a third large tattooed man, apparently just hanging out. They seemed baffled to see me.

Then I saw a mother and her middle-school-aged son sitting on a couch, waiting their turn. I didn't look like the rest of the clientele, and I was far older— even the mom seemed a decade younger than I am—but I still had my hand on the doorknob, so I had to do something. I could have turned and left them in peace, but instead I asked, "Is it first come, first served?"

"Yup," the barber said.

I sat on the couch, a wide and lowslung black leather model, and began watching "SportsCenter" on the flatscreen TV mounted near the ceiling. Loud hip-hop overwhelmed the room.

I could tell that the three men were wondering why I was there, but they got back to talking among themselves, and, in an effort to disappear and to put them at ease, I watched "SportsCenter" so intensely I must have looked as though I were listening for coded messages from space.

There were some hugs and backslaps when the occupant of the barber's chair stood up, and then the boy took his turn. The barber, in the meantime, had changed the TV channel to a reality show called "World's Dumbest Criminals."

The mom and I laughed at the show, which was periodically very funny, and then she lifted her chin at me and said, "You're up." The barber had carved an elaborate geometric design into the hair on the lower part of the boy's head. It had been done with a confident hand, and the boy was thrilled. He and his mother left, and I sat down. The man who'd got a haircut was leaning against the counter where all the gels and combs and washes were kept. The man in the other chair crossed his arms, revealing a pair of tattoos: "Family" on one arm, "First" on the other.

"So what's it gonna be?" the barber asked.

He was looking at the back of my head, and his two friends were looking at me. I told them it had been twenty-two years since I'd had a professional haircut.

"Looks like it," the barber said, and we all chuckled. "How come?"

I explained the budgetary benefits of cutting one's own hair, and the guys all nodded.

"I gotta come in here once a week," Family First said. He turned his head side to side, revealing an intricate design that would require regular upkeep. It was the work of an artist.

I told the barber to just take an inch off anywhere he saw the need, and he got started. Another man entered, athletic and tanned, with an array of tattoos on his arms. He sat under "World's Dumbest Criminals" and talked with the barber about an upcoming U.F.C. fight in Sacramento.

Then the barber turned to me. "So how'd you hear about this place?" He said this with a mixture of nonchalance and wariness. It was the question his two friends had been waiting for. Even the guy on the couch turned around.

I told them the story about T. S. Hawkins coming to this land, about how he built the former hospital where we were sitting, that the structure was dedicated to his granddaughter who had died young. All four men nodded respectfully.

Then something happened. The TV was on loud, and there was the stereo, too, so I heard nothing new, but the two friends were suddenly wondering what a certain sound was.

"Hear that?" the one with the new haircut said.

"Hear it?" Family First said. "Is that you?" he asked me.

I didn't know what they were talking about. The men said something about some ring or some electronic sound they'd just heard.

"Is someone here wearing a wire?" Family First asked. His friend laughed and patted himself down briefly, running his hands over his chest and ample stomach. Now they were looking at me again, and it finally dawned on me that they thought I was a narc.

"Aw, man," the barber said, about the possibility that I was wearing a wire. "I'd be out the window, I don't care."

The three of them discussed what they'd do if cops showed up, or were already in the room. I suddenly remembered the sign in front of the building, indicating that trespassers would be shot, sent to Heaven, etc. The atmosphere was still lighthearted, but the three friends around me were uncomfortable. It was odd: they continued to be polite to me, and my hair was being cut with great care, all while they were talking about the possible narc in the room as if he were some other person—not me.

Trying to change the subject, I asked Family First and his friend where they were from. Only then did I realize it was the kind of awkward question that a normal person would not ask but that a narc would find brilliant. One of the guys said he was from Visalia. The other didn't answer. The barber tilted my head down to work on the back of my neck. When I tilted my head up again, the two friends had gone.

The silence stretched out, and I decided to fill it. I asked the barber how long he'd been in Hollister.

"I don't know. Not long," he said.

"You like it here?" I asked. "Nah," he said. "It sucks."

He said he was from Gilroy, and he liked it much better there. Gilroy is not a booming metropolis—except maybe during the garlic festival—and is only fifteen miles away, but it's bigger than Hollister, and that's what mattered to him.

I asked him how he'd chosen the former Hazel Hawkins Memorial Hospital as the location for his barbershop, and he shrugged. The rent was cheap enough, he said. I asked how he stayed in business when there was no sign facing the street. Except for the doormat, there was no sign at all, come to think of it. He said that he had enough customers through word of mouth. I said something about the building having charm and history, but he didn't like the building, either.

"You know there was a coroner's office in the basement?"

he asked. For him, this was another reason to leave. He believed the building was haunted.

With the utmost professionalism, he trimmed around my ears and brushed the hair from my neck. He removed the bib. The haircut was fifteen dollars, and I paid him and thanked him—the haircut was flawless—but we were both very confused about all that had just transpired.

"See you in another ten years," he said. I was halfway through the door when he added, cheerfully, "I probably won't be here then, though."

Hollister, like many towns of its size and socioeconomics, has been affected by gang activity and by the related spike in meth and heroin use. The town had been discussing the possibility of adding police officers to address the drug trade and the gang presence. Maybe the barber thought I was one of these new cops—and he'd assumed that I'd made assumptions about him and his friends. I thought about going back to apologize, but wouldn't that be exactly what a narc would do?

Gang activity, real and imagined, has a historical echo in Hollister. In the early part of the twentieth century, the American Motorcyclist Association started the Gypsy Tours, for which bikers were encouraged to hold races, rallies, shows, and picnics. During the Second World War, the rallies were suspended, but afterward they were revived. The atmosphere, though, was different. Many of the young men returning from Europe and the Pacific were shattered, disillusioned. Men who otherwise would have expected to stay in their rural homes or work in urban factories had now seen the world, had seen unnameable horrors, and were no longer beholden to pedestrian life paths. Motorcycling became more popular than ever, and the rallies became bigger and wilder.

And so, on July 4, 1947, the Gypsy Tour descended on Hollister, and, by some estimates, the town's population of forty-five hundred doubled overnight, with all kinds of clubs—the Boozefighters, the Market Street Commandos, the Galloping Goose, the Pissed Off Bastards of Bloomington. The members rode through town, making noise, drinking beer, breaking bottles, and generally causing low-level mayhem. Police struggled to control the crowds.

Rumors of the unruly bikers morphed into rumors of rioting, and six years later Marlon Brando was playing a confused and misunderstood leather-clad young man, caught up in a riot in Hollister. "The Wild One" terrified law-abiding citizens, but to rebellious bike-riding men it seemed like a blueprint for life. Soon enough, the Hells Angels took note, and they began to attend yearly gatherings, although the locals were divided on the advantages of their patronage. In any case, the town saw fit, in 1997, to commemorate the "riot" of 1947 with a fiftieth-anniversary party.

The celebrations have continued over the years, only occasionally called off owing to lack of interest or the fluctuating tolerance of the town. Debbie Taylor was quick to point out that though the rally hadn't happened the year before, they were planning to reinstate it. "Definitely next year," she said. (There was indeed a rally the following year, but it would be Debbie Taylor's last. She's moved on from the chamber of commerce and away from Hollister. Eli's Chop Shop is now closed, too.)

After I left the chamber of commerce, I meandered through the town, passing Hazel Street and Hawkins Street and Steinbeck Street, and the middle school and the high school, the students, most of them Latino, finishing the day and heading home. The afternoon was aging, and I figured it was time to make my way to the modern incarnation of the hospital. Only then did I realize that I hadn't come across one person, all day, wearing the Hollister name. It seemed like a remarkable inversion: anywhere else in the world, seeing thousands of kids leaving school, you'd see the word "Hollister" on someone's chest or hat or shorts. But here, where the word might mean the most, you don't see it at all.

When I got to the hospital, the sun was setting and the shock was real. The complex was large and modern. Signs everywhere featured the name Hazel Hawkins prominently. And the new women's center was a gleaming addition, with its own roundabout and a two-story atrium.

Already there were a few dozen people gathered, all of them well dressed. I was wearing shorts and a torn brown brandless hoodie. I walked in, carrying my copy of *Some Recollections*, with pages of Hazel and T.S. flagged. And then, moving among the attendees in their suits and dresses, I realized with great clarity that I was that peculiar relative: the poorly dressed and unshaven man who shows up carrying a hundred-year-old book with certain pages marked. My new haircut, given to me by a man who thought I was a cop, was the only thing that made me look presentable or sane.

I saw Debbie Taylor. She introduced me to a number of doctors and dignitaries, always as the descendant of Hazel Hawkins. Most of them didn't know the story behind the name and were even more surprised to hear that Hazel Hawkins was a child when she left this world. I told truncated versions of the tale, always pointing to the book, trying not to appear as unhinged as I looked.

Otherwise, the ceremony was practical and funny and joyous. Gloria Torres, the hospital's director of Maternal and Child Health, said that this new facility was what the community needed and deserved—she called the complex's previous birthing center "embarrassing." Gordon Machado, the president of the San Benito Health Care District Board, noted that the construction was done by local labor, and this news received some sturdy applause. The project manager, Liam McCool, was introduced, after Machado joked that though he was Irish, McCool showed up every morning, even the day after St. Patrick's. McCool waved and smiled at the audience, whose diversity reflected the particular blend of people in today's Central Valley: there were the older, whiter representatives, there were the second and third-generation Latino families whose parents were laborers and whose children will be college graduates, there were nurses and doctors who had immigrated from India and China and beyond.

There are those who think that California is a state where Spanish speakers should have natural sway. And there are those who think that this is a state where English speakers have preeminence, and there are those who insist that if we have any sense of history, of decency, the native peoples of California should be given the first seat at the table. And then there are those who have no idea at all about the history of the state and do not care.

But California has always been a state of visitors, of late arrivals, of seekers innocent and not so innocent. Though it might not be good enough for a Hollister clothing outlet, this is the real Hollister, a place where people work hard and sometimes struggle with their past and their present but look with great practicality toward the future. They build new hospitals that will bring new Californians into the world, new hospitals named after a young white pioneer child few ever knew existed.

Dave Eggers is the author of many novels and works of nonfiction, including The Circle, What Is the What, *finalist for the National Book Critics Circle Award, and* A Hologram for the King, *finalist for the National Book Award. He lives in Northern California with his family.*

SOME RECOLLECTIONS OF A BUSY LIFE

by T.S. HAWKINS

CHAPTER ONE

CONDITIONS IN THE "FAR WEST" SEVENTY YEARS AGO

IN WRITING THESE RECOLLECTIONS, I do so, not expecting or believing that there has been anything in my life that would be of interest to the general public. I trust, however, that my children and grandchildren, and their descendants, and a very few dear friends, may desire to know something of the great changes that have taken place in the manner of living in the last seventy years, as well as something of the hardships and privations through which their forefathers passed in that part of our country which was then known as the "Far West."

It may be well in the beginning to describe some of the conditions surrounding my own home, as well as those of most of the people residing in country districts west of the Mississippi River.

To begin with, we had no railroads, no telegraphic or telephonic communication with the outer world. News of events transpiring in the East took weeks in reaching us, and the small weekly papers, which were all we had, gave us very sparing reports of what had happened in Europe months before. Electrical lighting was a thing undreamed of. Even coal oil and coal-oil lamps were then unknown. We had no cook stoves and not even a match. Like the Sun worshippers, we were always expected to have a live coal on our altars. When the family retired for the night, the fire was carefully covered with embers and if by accident it should go out, one of the children was sent to a neighbor to borrow or else a little powder was poured into the old Kentucky rifle, some "tow" rammed down on it, and this was fired out against the wall, where paper and shavings were prepared to receive it; being thence transferred to the open fireplace, where it was cared for until a good blaze was finally started.

Every house had a large open fireplace equipped with a swinging crane, where all the roasting was done. I do not think anything better for roasting was ever invented than the old-fashioned crane. There was a large hearth, where coals were drawn from the fireplace for the broiling iron, or for the large cast iron ovens in which the baking was done. These ovens were raised from the hearth on three legs so that live coals could be placed under them, and the lid of the oven had a rim an inch or more high raised around it, so that the coals placed on top would not fall off, and thus heat was applied both above and below.

For lights, we had pine knots or candles, and such candles! When I can first remember, such a thing as a candle mold was unknown. The candles were made by melting tallow in a large cauldron, with a certain portion of water, and if something extra was desired, beeswax was added. Then a dozen pieces of candle wick of the right length for a candle were doubled over a rod and let down into the cauldron, again raised into the air until the tallow adhering to the wicks became hardened. Then they were again let down and raised into the air, this process being repeated until the candle had grown to about the right size, when it was taken from the rod and other wicks substituted until the tallow was all removed from the surface of the water. Such candles were not artistically a success. Sometimes they would be the largest at the wrong end and they were always lumpy. Sometimes more tallow would harden on one side of the wick than the other and the wick would not be in the center. Still they gave a fairly good light.

Such a thing as "store" soap was unknown. The ashes from the fires were carefully preserved during the winter, and in the spring when "soap-making time" came, an ash-hopper was constructed from boards, with a trough at the bottom. Into this hopper the ashes were thrown until it was full; then water was poured on, and in a few hours it would percolate through the ashes and come out of the trough at the bottom the strongest kind of lye. This was caught in wooden vessels, and poured into a large cast iron kettle. To this was added all kinds of waste fat, which had been preserved during the year. A fire was built under the kettle and kept boiling until the mixture reached the proper consistency, when it was put away in barrels for the year. It was pretty strong, almost to the point of taking the skin off, but its cleansing properties were, I suppose, equal to that of any of the finer soaps of today. This was the original of all the "soft soap" I ever heard of, and I think very much superior and a very different article from the kind I have sometimes had handed out to me even to the present day.

There were no brick or frame houses in the neighborhood where we lived. The house of my earliest recollection, and in which I was born, was rather a superior building and consisted of two detached one-and-a-half-story log houses placed twelve or fourteen feet apart, one roof covering the whole. The buildings were of hewed logs, the spaces between the logs being "chinked" with thin pieces of limestone and then plastered over with lime.

There were small windows of twelve panes of eight by ten-inch glass. At one end was built a large stone chimney, running up outside of the building, with an immense fireplace and hearth inside. The passage between the two houses was left open at both ends and was a delightfully cool place to sit on hot summer days. I do not remember any house being divided into rooms. I recall a neighbor, with a family of some eight children from two to twenty years of age, whose log cabin consisted of one immense room, perhaps twenty-five feet square, without a single partition. They cooked, ate and slept all in the one room.

When quite a large boy I occasionally went home with one of the neighbor boys to stay all night. It was an awful trial to me when bedtime came, being, I imagine, both timid and diffident. The men and boys would go outside until the women and girls were safely in bed, then we would go in, and when we had located ourselves the light would be put out and we would undress and get into bed in the dark. It looks crude to us in this enlightened day, but it was the best the people could do with the few tools they possessed at that time. Of one thing I am sure, the inconvenience did not lessen the modesty of either sex, and I have never known of purer-minded or a cleaner lot of young people anywhere.

In our home we had a stairway leading to the upper part of the house where we boys slept. The roof of clapboards was only a little above our heads, and the patter of the rain on the roof on summer nights is among my most pleasant recollections. The boards made a good roof to turn off the rain, but in the winter when the wind blew the fine snow would drift through the interstices between the boards of the roof. It was glorious up in the old-fashioned feather bed, with the blankets pulled up to one's ears, listening to the roar of the wind, the pelting of the hail and snow and the war of the elements, until one fell asleep.

In the morning we would awake to find the bedding and the floor covered an inch or more in drifted snow. And woe to the boy who was dilatory in rising, for those who were up first would take the bed-clothes with them, and in their place the lazy ones would be covered with hands full of snow. It was equal to an electric shock to get a boy out of bed. It seems at this distance a rough life; but I do not remember that we ever considered it so, and it certainly served to make one hardy and self-reliant.

Our clothing was all home made. We raised a small field of flax, which at the proper season was cut and spread out in the field to be rotted by the dew, or, better still, in a shallow pond of water if convenient. Here it would lie until the wood fiber was thoroughly rotted, when it was taken out and spread on the ground until dry. Next it was taken to the "break," when all the woody substance was broken to pieces, and largely removed, and then to the "skutching" board, where the remainder was removed from the fiber, and the fiber beaten very fine. It was then ready for the women to spin. This was done by placing the cleaned fiber on the distaff of a small spinning wheel at which the operator sat, working it with her feet, something like the modern sewing machine, while her hands were free to manipulate the flax and draw it out into fine and even threads. These threads were then wound on to large spools, then transferred to the "winding yards," where it was made into "skeins," then to the old hand loom, where it was woven into linen for summer clothing and for various household uses. We were not arrayed in fine linen, but it certainly was comfortable and almost everlasting.

We also kept a small flock of sheep and at the proper season they were shorn; the wool was washed to free it from dirt and animal grease. It was then "picked" by hand. This was a tedious process, as every particle was taken apart and all the burrs and other matter removed, and was largely done of evenings when all the family could take part; the men and boys could help while they were resting. There was always considerable emulation as to who should have the largest and cleanest pile.

This cleaned wool was made into "rolls" by using a pair of hand cards. It was now ready for spinning. This was done on a large spinning-wheel. The end of a roll was attached to the spindle, and the large wheel was turned swiftly and when it had acquired sufficient momentum the operator would walk back briskly the full length of the room, drawing the thread out through her fingers until it had reached a proper fineness, and when it was sufficiently twisted, the wheel was reversed and the thread run up on the spindle. Another roll would be attached to the end of the thread and the same process repeated until the spindle was full. I have often wondered how many miles a girl would walk in a day of twelve or fourteen hours, back and forth. I imagine it would tire any of the athletes of the present day.

Then the thread was unwound from the spindle on to the "winding yards" and taken off in "skeins."

It was then ready for coloring. For our common clothes, the bark of various trees was used. I think oak, walnut and butternut for different colors. For our best suits, wool dyed in indigo to a deep blue and then thoroughly mixed with pure white was used, making what was called blue mixed jeans, which was the very top of the fashion. This woolen thread was next woven into cloth on the hand loom, in a manner similar to that already described for linen.

Our farming was of a very primitive character. Our plows consisted of an iron shear and wooden mold-board. We raised Indian corn, some wheat, and a small field of tobacco, and an abundance of all kinds of vegetables. Corn was used in various forms in the family for bread, being one of our principal foods, followed in importance only by "hog and hominy," which was a close second.

The only mills consisted of a pair of stones propelled by

horse power on an inclined wheel. When we had to go to mill a long sack was filled with corn and placed on the back of a horse, and a boy on top of the sack leading another horse. We generally joined with a neighbor with another sack, another boy, and another led horse, as it took four horses to turn the wheel.

Arriving at the mill, if no one was ahead of us, the miller took our sacks of corn and, after taking out his toll, placed the balance in the hopper. In the meantime we would lead the horses on to the wheel, the wheel would start, the mill stones would revolve and, if you had good luck, by night you would reach home with your sack of meal.

We always took our sacks fairly full of corn, but I have heard of people who filled only one end with corn and placed a large stone in the other to balance, but I do not know if this was true. At least it must have been before my day when people were less enlightened.

One thing I remember well is, that to ride a well-filled sack of corn on a bareback horse four or five miles to mill, without it falling off, was a difficult task. I know of nothing more heartbreaking than a couple of twelve-year-old boys trying to boost a limp sack of corn back onto the horse from whence it had fallen. How I have perspired and worked and prayed for someone stronger to come by to help us in our difficulty. If a sack of corn has no reasoning faculties I cannot understand why every individual grain always wanted to get into the heavier end.

There were no butchers or butcher shops and the larger part of the year we had bacon and ham three times a day. Once in a while the neighbors would band together and kill a beef and divide it among themselves; but in the summer time fresh meat would only keep a very short time in that moist, warm climate, and cold storage was unknown.

About the last of December "hog-killing" time would begin. This generally lasted two months. The hams, shoulders and sides were salted down and after a time were taken up and smoked, while we lived for months on backbones, spare ribs and sausage. We just had to eat them to keep them from spoiling. At first I used to think nothing on earth tasted so good as a nice broiled spare rib, or fresh sausage, or the tenderloin around the backbone, but after a month or two of such diet, even in mid-winter, one wouldn't dare look a live hog in the face.

I would not have the reader infer that we had no other kinds of food, for that would be untrue. There was an abundance of all kinds of wild animals, which we could have for the taking. The conservation of wild game was unknown, and no one ever seemed to dream that it would not last forever.

In the spring when the tender buds came out on the elm and other trees, the young half-grown tree squirrels would appear, also, and were easily killed. Deer were plentiful and there was no closed season.

The woods were full of wild turkeys and in the fall they would come into the stubble-fields, bringing their half-grown young by the hundreds. From experience I can say that the tender breast of a half-grown turkey nicely broiled is something to be remembered.

Then there were quail by the thousands, and after the snow had fallen, we boys would go out by the straw-stacks and clear away the snow from the ground for a few feet square; over the clear space we would set a light trap built of lath, with a figure-four trigger. Over the trap would be thrown a little straw and a little wheat scattered under it. Often in the evening we would find from one to two dozen quail safely caught.

In telling hunting and game stories, one must be careful not to exaggerate. I began with hundreds of wild turkeys, thousands of quail and now wonder if the figures will hold out and tell the truth. I hope so.

In the winter the prairie chickens would come in by the hundreds of thousands. The fields and the prairie were literally alive with them. I remember my father going out in front of the house and shooting them off the roof. At other times wild geese were just as numerous as the prairie chicken.

I hardly know if it is safe to risk my veracity by telling you the actual truth about the wild pigeons. In the fall of the year they would come in by the millions. In the afternoon the heavens would be darkened and the sun obscured for hours, as they flew over our heads toward their roosting place.

With my father I once visited one of those roosting places, a few miles from our home. The pigeon has certain places where they go to roost year after year. This one was a heavily wooded area covering over a thousand acres of large forest trees. We arrived about an hour before sunset, and soon they began to arrive.

They would alight on a great forest tree, covering every branch, and then light on each other until the branches would snap, falling to the ground, while the birds would rise with a sound like thunder and seek another location. As it grew toward the dusk, of the evening, the noise of falling branches and the thunder of millions of wings was simply terrifying. People went for miles to see and hear. A gun was not necessary; anyone could knock over with a pole as many as he cared to carry home. I visited this forest a few years later when the birds had left the place, and it looked as though it had been swept by a tornado.

While writing of game, it would never do to pass over the luscious opossum. All epicures in the South, without regard to "race, color or previous condition of servitude," have from time immemorial considered a nice roast 'possum with sweet potatoes the "piece de resistance" at any banquet. Although

I have often sat at a table and heard all extolling its excellency, I must acknowledge that I never could screw up sufficient courage to taste it.

Many a night after a hard day's work I have roamed the river bottoms with other boys and a pack of hounds hunting him. Of all animals he is most "child-like and bland." Often when the hounds would bay informing us that they had "treed" something, when we reached the place we would see from one to three or four 'possums, just out of the dogs' reach, with their long prehensile tails wound around a branch of a tree, with their eyes closed and swinging back and forth with the breeze, apparently as unconcerned as though there was not a boy or a dog in a hundred miles. He certainly can "play 'possum" to the limit. You can strike him, throw him on the ground, stick a coal of fire to his tail, and he will sleep on just as unconsciously as ever. And what a happy animal he must be. When bedtime comes, all he has to do is to find the branch of a tree, about the right size for him, wrap his tail around it half a dozen times, let go and swing off, where he will sleep the long night through.

It seems proper for me to say before I pass on that I never was a mighty hunter. My father and my brother, next younger than myself, were both very fond of the sport, but, though a good shot, I preferred practicing at a mark rather than at live animals.

Money was almost unknown among us. I remember when a boy I was sent to the post office in Palmyra, some six miles distant, where I found two letters. This was before the days of postage stamps. On one of these letters there was due fifteen cents, and on the other ten cents postage. As I did not have the money I had to go home without them. I recollect there was a good deal of skirmishing around among the neighbors to raise the amount, so that I could go back after the letters. I mention this incident only to illustrate how scarce ready money was with us, for we were as well off, and perhaps better than the average people in the community. Yet we had an abundance of everything else and lived well. Whenever the groceries and provisions were running low, the wagon would be loaded with hams, bacon and tobacco and my father would drive to Hannibal, and barter for a supply of everything needed to last for months. Butter, eggs, poultry and vegetables were raised on the farm.

Occasionally, perhaps once a week, we had wheaten bread; at all other times, corn in its various forms was used. I imagine the reason why bread from wheat was so seldom used was because of the difficulty of raising and preparing wheat without machinery.

When the wheat was ready to harvest, men went into the fields with "cradles," with which they cut the ripened grain. Others followed, who raked it up and bound it into bundles.

It was then "shocked," that is, about a dozen bundles were placed together, heads upward, while one or two other bundles were broken across the center of the straw, and placed over the standing bundles, forming a cap which was almost impervious to the rain. Later on the bundles were hauled to the barn or stacked around the threshing floor.

Those who only farmed a few acres, placed the bundles on an open platform, where the grain was beaten out with "flails," the grain falling through the interstices between the rails and the straw when the grain was all beaten out, was removed.

Those who raised larger crops had a threshing floor. In some instances these were in the barn, but usually a place was leveled off on the open ground, then trodden as solidly as possible. On this floor the bundles of grain were placed, the heads all pointing in one direction, and the bands cut. Then the boys mounted on one horse and leading another were turned on, usually four boys and eight horses, and traveled around and around for hours, while the men would shake up the straw with pitch forks, and from time to time remove that from which the grain had all been extracted.

It was weary work for the boys and the horses. Imagine sitting astride of a raw-boned perspiring horse, without saddle or blanket, for hours and hours, going around and around a circle not more than forty feet in diameter, until one grows dizzy and sick. Instead of traveling unceasingly around the small circle, you would suddenly be standing still and the world would commence whirling around in the opposite direction until at least one boy I knew would fall almost senseless into the straw at the horse's feet, only to be shaken up and lifted on the horse's back, to go on again in the interminable round.

It was not funny to be a sensitive, imaginative boy in those days. I think my early experience on the threshing floor has made me always impatient with men and women, too, who always seem to be traveling in a circle and arriving nowhere in the end.

After the straw was all removed from the threshing floor, and the grain and chaff swept into a pile in the center, the floor was again filled with bundles and the same process repeated until the grain was all threshed and gathered with the chaff into one large pile. Then the old "fanning mill" was brought out, and while one man turned the handle another filled the hopper with a scoop shovel. The chaff was blown out and the wheat fell on an inclined plane and ran down on to a piece of canvas, from which it was placed in sacks and perhaps run through the fanning mill two or three times before it was thoroughly cleaned and ready for market.

This seems a slow process when compared with the combined harvester of today, which goes into a field of standing grain, cuts, threshes and sacks it, ready for market, all in one operation. But this was the only way the western people knew seventy years ago.

I am glad of the improvement, if for no other reason than to keep the boys of this generation from going round and round forever on that old threshing floor. And yet, sometimes when some of the wise young people come around with their cocksureness and immeasurable knowledge of everything under the sun, I feel as if I would enjoy boosting them astride old Bill's prominent backbone and have them try it for an hour or two. I am sure it would bring them to a more humble view of their importance. But it is time to drop these descriptions and get down to the more serious task of giving the reader, as far as possible from my own recollections, some of the principal events of a long and busy life.

CHAPTER TWO

SOME REMEMBERED INCIDENTS OF EARLY CHILDHOOD

I WAS born on a farm in Marion County, Missouri, on the sixth day of March, 1836, my father having been married in Cynthiana, Kentucky, in March two years before, and with the usual desire of the young to go West, had traveled the five hundred miles overland through the States of Kentucky, Ohio, Indiana and Illinois to their new home, a journey of about a month. Our old farm was about six miles from Palmyra, the County Seat, and twelve miles from Hannibal City, on the Mississippi River. It was a small village at that time, now grown into a thriving city.

My family had always been farmers, or planters, as they are called in the South. My grandfather came from Virginia to Kentucky somewhere about 1800. I clearly remember some of his stories, and as a small boy, was particularly interested in his telling me how they lived in blockhouses and were in constant fear of the Indians, with whom the early settlers had many conflicts. No one ever went outside the gates without a gun.

Grandfather used to tell of an old man who was a strong fatalist, his theory being that whatever is to be will be. One day the old gentleman wished to visit a neighboring fort, but when he was ready to start, he found that one of the boys had carried off his gun, so he concluded to give up the visit for that day. One of his friends said to him: "Why do you not go without your gun? If there are any Indians in hiding, according to your doctrine, they could not kill you if your time had not come." "Yes," said the old fatalist, "that is true, but suppose I should meet an Indian and his time had come? It wouldn't do not to have my rifle." I believe I have read something like this somewhere, but I have no doubt this was the original version.

There were many obstacles to be overcome by the settlers of grandfather's time, and as a sample of the difficulties under which they lived, he told me that at a certain season of the year the men from different stations would meet together at an appointed rendezvous to the number of two or three hundred, all armed to the teeth, and with wagons and big kettles and other necessary utensils, they would proceed in regular

SOME REMEMBERED INCIDENTS OF EARLY CHILDHOOD

army order some eighty miles to certain salt springs, where, while someone stood guard day and night, others cut wood and others boiled the salt water in the big kettles. This would continue two or three weeks, when they would each have secured a small sack of salt to last them for a year. Then they would return home in the same order as they came.

These salt springs were right in the favorite hunting grounds of the Indians and many battles were fought for their possession.

My father's family came over early in the settlement of Virginia and from there many branches scattered into Kentucky and Tennessee. My grandfather married a young lady from near the White Sulphur Springs, in Virginia, and resided near Havre de Grace, in Maryland, before removing to Kentucky.

My father was born on the old homestead near Cynthiana, Ky., on January 1st, 1811, where he grew to manhood, and was married to Miss Margaretta Frazer in 1834. My mother's father was of Scotch descent, as the name implies, and was born in Virginia in 1776, while my maternal grandmother's family (the Millers) came originally from the North of Ireland. I have an impression that they were a family of some importance, as the younger members that I knew later on were rather superior people.

I remember my Grandmother Frazer as one of the most gracious women I ever knew, with all the old-time polish and courtesy that distinguished the women of that day.

It will be seen from the above that I have English, Scotch and Irish blood in my veins.

In looking back over the more than seventy years that have intervened, and gathering up the threads of events long past, so many incidents of my early childhood come back to me that I am confused and hardly know where to begin.

The first distinct recollection—the farthest back that I can go—is of an incident that must have occurred when I was a little over four years of age.

I think it must have been in June or July of 1840 that my father took me with him to Hannibal. It must have been some kind of a gathering of the Whig party. It was during the campaign in which Harrison was elected President. I remember seeing a great many men wearing bell-crowned hats, with a log cabin, formed of some kind of light wood, built up from the brim, with a tiny door, and the latch-string hanging out. (Since writing the above, I have seen in the *Century* magazine some pictures of the campaign of 1840, where the same kind of men and hats are produced, but the log cabin is left out. It is a pity that the artist had not known of them, as they would have added interest to the picture.) We think now that a Presidential election creates a great deal of excitement, but I imagine it is nothing when compared to the one, the slogan of which was "Tippecanoe and Tyler too."

SOME REMEMBERED INCIDENTS OF EARLY CHILDHOOD

On this visit I saw for the first time the "Great Father of Waters," and the steamboats going up and down or lying at the wharves. There were also a large number of painted Indians clad in blankets and their black hair adorned with creations of eagle feathers. I remember how scared I was, and I did not know how soon they would be after my scalp.

I was a healthy, hardy boy, and loved to be out of doors, and only a little later than the incident described, I would follow my father to the field when they were "laying by" the corn, that is, the last plowing, when the stalks are large and strong and the tassels just beginning to appear, and standing well over the horses' backs.

My father used to lift me up astride the old horse, and I would hang on to the "hames" and ride back and forth all day long. Sometimes I would fall asleep and tumble off, but the plowed ground was soft and it did not hurt, and only stopped operations long enough for me to be picked up, now wide awake, and be put back on the old horse again. Perhaps the lapse of years and my imagination have exaggerated how often this would happen, but it seems to me now that I spent the whole day in the hot August sun, going to sleep every few furrows, falling off, waking up, falling off, waking up, and going to sleep and falling off again.

I looked with a good deal of contempt on my younger brother, who was content to lie down at the end of the row on my father's coat under the shade of a tree and sleep quietly while I rode in the hot sun through the long rows of corn. Looking backwards after so many years I can see that I must have been only a nuisance and that my brother was more of a philosopher than I.

How proud I was when first permitted to ride the horses to water. It seems to me that instead of everything being arranged for convenience, as we have it now, that the people studied to make things as inconvenient as possible. Our house and barn stood on a commanding elevation, a beautiful view, but at least a quarter of a mile from the nearest water. Thinking it over this may have been to get above the malaria, which was prevalent at this early date, nearly everyone shaking a month or two each fall with chills and fever.

The watering place was in what was called the "Big Branch." This little stream went dry in summer except in one place known as the "round hole." I suppose it was fed by springs, as it always stood at the same level. It was some forty feet long and twenty feet across, and obtained a depth of three feet in the center. It was shaded by an immense oak, which grew on the bank and spread its huge branches low over the water.

To this place I was allowed to ride one horse, leading another, when they would go in up to their knees and drink their fill, then we would return to the barn and give them their feed. One very hot summer day the horse I was riding was not content to stop at the usual place, but in spite of all I could do, went deliberately toward the deepest part, right under a large branch of the tree that just cleared his back, while I was scraped off as though I had been a fly, and found myself strangling for breath when I could get my head above the water. Everyone said I might have been drowned, and it was decided that I should not go again, but I begged so hard that I guess they must have relented, for I kept on riding the horses to water. I had a cousin named Joe Snell, who lived just one mile from us. He was four years older than I, and sometimes came to see us and help my father with his work. It must have been about a year after I received my ducking that it was arranged for me to go home with him and stay all night. We were to ride the same old "Bill." We started just as it was growing dark. The road was only a path cut through the thick brush and overhung by large trees.

We had proceeded about a quarter of a mile, Joe riding in front and I behind. Suddenly some yards in front of us an apparition stepped from the brush. It was clothed in white and about eight feet high. The Thing walked slowly down the road in front of us, emitting the most dismal groans and bloodcurdling shrieks.

Joe was scared, the old horse was scared, and I? Well, it was the first ghost I had even seen and I was terrified beyond expression. The horse wanted to turn tail and run for home, but scared as we were, we would rather have faced a hundred ghosts than to have gone back with a story of that kind.

Finally the Thing moved slowly into an opening in the brush and we both kicked with our heels and belabored the horse in every way we could, and shot by the ghost. With a terrible yell, it rushed out at us as we passed and nearly caught the bridle; but we got by, and it followed us for quite a distance with groans and yells, when it apparently gave up the chase and we saw it no more.

Now, Bill was an old, a very old, horse, and he could not gallop or run; nothing but trot, trot—it seemed to me just up and down almost in one place. We proceeded in this way for some distance, when the jolting and the scare gave me such a pain in my side that I begged to let him walk, even if the ghost was following us.

We proceeded without further incident until we were passing alongside of an old field rail fence near his home. The fence was hidden by a second growth of brush that had grown up in the fence corners. Suddenly from almost beneath us we heard a terrible noise and threshing in the undergrowth, and with a whoof! whoof! a huge wild animal rushed out directly under the horse's feet.

The old horse suddenly sidestepped and left us rolling on the ground, while he really ran on to the house. We lost no time in gathering ourselves up and following him. In our imagination we could hear the wild animal panting at our heels. We, however, reached the house, alive, dusty, scratched and bruised, but very courageous, now that the danger was over. It was indeed a wonderful adventure, and very real to me.

On investigation the next morning, we found the wild animal was a harmless old sow, which, with her litter of pigs, had established her comfortable home in the corner of the fence under the brush. Later on it leaked out that the ghost was the hired man, who had put his hat on a pole to give him greater height, and had wrapped it and himself in a white sheet, and with the deliberate intention of giving us a fright, had waited for us.

I would not be surprised if most of the ghost stories we read about have no more real foundation than this.

CHAPTER THREE

THE LOG SCHOOLHOUSE OF BOYHOOD DAYS

IT MUST HAVE BEEN shortly after my seventh birthday that I started to my first school. A neighbor boy came by for me. We went by a blazed path through the woods, crossing the South River on a fallen tree, and climbed a long hill to the schoolhouse, two miles from my home. Many of the pupils had to go a much greater distance. The schoolhouse was situated at least a mile from any residence and on a level piece of land on the summit of a long ridge.

A little further on was a log church belonging to the Baptists, and the place was known as "Pleasant Hill." The schoolhouse was built of logs, with a "puncheon" floor. A puncheon floor is made from some kind of soft wood, generally a linn tree, which is cut down and split into slabs about a foot or more wide and three or four inches thick. One side was dressed off with an adz until it was fairly smooth, and the under side was notched where they lay over the floor joists, until the top was level. This made a durable and very solid floor.

A log was cut out of the wall on one side at about four or five feet from the floor and extending along one side of the building. Just below this opening a board was fixed which was called the writing-board. There were no desks with backs and all the comforts of today. The seats were made by cutting down a tree ten or twelve inches in diameter, splitting it in halves and smoothing off the surface on the split side. Then two holes were bored near each end with a large auger, in the round side and at the proper angle. Next legs were split out about two inches in diameter, and from two to three feet long. One end of these legs was shaved down to the proper size and driven into the holes already bored. Turn it with the legs down and your bench is ready to climb on, and would accommodate a half dozen boys. Imagine a seven-year-old boy shinning up one of the legs and carefully hitching along the bench until he reached his place. Then imagine him sitting there with his feet dangling a foot or two from the floor, with no back to lean against, from eight o'clock in the morning until five or six in the evening, except the two hours at noon.

Teachers were supposed to open school as early as they could after breakfast and close only in time for the children to get home before dark. The length of the school day depended entirely on the season of the year. There was always a "play time" from twelve to two. I am not sure, however, that we always had the two hours. There was a mark cut in the floor which always showed when twelve o'clock came, if the sun was shining, but of course the two o'clock had to be guessed at, as it could not be regulated by a mark as the noon hour was, and no teacher or pupil ever had a watch, and of course a clock in a schoolhouse was absurd. So I expect our play time depended largely on the state of the teacher's liver or, in the long summer days, on how soundly he slept the hours away.

The girls were required to sweep the floor and to clean up generally. The boys were required to bring the water from the spring, a quarter of a mile away. They also gathered in the down timber from the forest, cut it into lengths for the enormous fireplace, and in the winter carry it in and keep the fire going.

The teaching was the old A, B, C way, and a child just starting in would sit on one of these benches eight hours a day, with a primer in which he did not know a letter, only to be called "off his perch" about four times a day, to go up to the teacher and try to tell him the names of the characters. It seems to me now that it was inhuman and barbarous, and I wonder why everyone did not have curvature of the spine.

I think I had picked up the alphabet somehow before

starting to school. In fact, I cannot remember a time when I could not pick out words in the weekly newspaper which came to our house. On the other hand I have known children to go regularly for a whole quarter, which was twelve weeks, before mastering the alphabet. I do not mean that I was brighter than others, but I always wanted to know why, and no labor was too great for me and no difficulties that I would not endeavor to surmount.

I do not recall anything worth mentioning for the next two or three years. I went to school when I could, shook with chills and fever for two or three months every fall, commenced being useful in various ways, doing chores, taking the horses to water, "tending the gap," etc. I have no doubt the reader will ask, "What is tending the gap?" The fields at this time were enclosed by a "worm fence," that is, a fence made of split rails ten feet long, and laid on top of one another at a sufficient angle to make a solid fence, the ends of each panel interlocking with the next.

There were no gates to these fields, and when the season for harvesting the crop had arrived the rails on two interlocking panels were opened so that the wagons could go in and out. As it took some time to open a gap, instead of closing it every time the wagon went in or out, a small boy was stationed there to keep the horses, hogs, cows and other animals from going through. It was a lazy enough job. I recall one day in the fall of 1843 that I was engaged in this task and, though not yet eight years of age, the circumstance comes back to me as though it were only yesterday.

For more than a year the Millerites, a sect preaching that the end of the world was at hand, had been busy formulating their doctrine and creating great excitement throughout all the country. Hundreds had embraced their teachings, and finally the leaders of the movement announced that they had proven from the Scriptures that at twelve o'clock on the day fixed the end of the world would surely come. Many people gave away all they possessed and were busy for days and weeks ahead preparing their ascension robes.

On the morning set, clothed in their white robes, they gathered on the summits of the hills, or in the open fields, where there was a good place to soar from on their, as yet unfledged, wings, and awaited the end.

Some way we must not have given it much attention, and, though I must have taken it all in, I was so much of a Missourian even then that they would have to "show me."

The appointed day must have been in September or October, and I was out by the fence minding the gap. My younger brother came wandering down to where I was. He evidently had not heard what a momentous day it was, and as I saw him coming I concluded there was a chance for some fun.

When he came near I said I thought he was home with

mother, and added that it was then eleven o'clock; that at exactly twelve the wise men had declared the world would come to an end; that all the good were going straight to heaven, and that the bad were to go the other way.

He looked at me for a moment and turning around he lit out for home. The farther he got the faster he ran, and every time he hit the ground he would let out a terrible and heart-rending yell. I sat there at my gap and laughed until I cried. Later on, when I went home, my mother gave me a good spanking. This time I cried without laughing. Looking back after all these years, I really feel no regrets, and think the fun was worth all I had to pay.

CHAPTER FOUR

A JOURNEY BY RIVER TO THE BLUE-GRASS COUNTRY

My life went on in the even tenor of its way for the next two or three years, when circumstances changed everything in our lives. My father had gone security in a large amount for a relative who was supposed to be wealthy, and who traded to New Orleans, taking down mules principally, and bringing back sugar, molasses and other products of the South. This relative suddenly failed and then died, leaving my father with a load of debt on his shoulders.

Without a murmur he sold our large farm and everything on it, and from the proceeds paid the last dollar of indebtedness he had assumed. He had reserved an eighty-acre tract, being nearly a mile from our home and running down to the South River.

There was on this piece of land some fifteen acres of cleared land, and no buildings of any kind. We had possession of the old home for six months, and in this time we had built a new house, not quite so good as our former home, but sufficient for our comfort, and with sufficient income for our needs, by using the strictest economy.

To add to our trouble, we had hardly settled before my father was taken sick with throat and lung troubles, which incapacitated him for active work, and for three years, from about 1849, I became the head of the working force on the little farm. I was now large enough to reach the handles of the plow and could make a hand in most all kinds of farm work.

I had only a few months of schooling each year, but, being a hard student, I kept up with my classes. From the age of thirteen to sixteen I developed a great love for reading, which has lasted me all my life, and has been the source of the greatest pleasure, as well as of benefit to me in many ways.

All my spare hours were devoted to reading such books as I could borrow, and it was a strange mixture I got. Books were very scarce then, but in one family I ran across a case of old books that had been printed in England and brought West by their owner from Virginia. I suppose they must have been a hundred years old. They were printed in old English type. The letter "S" was almost identical with "f," with the cross left off.

Among the works I read were those of Flavius Josephus, the great historian of the Jews, in five or six volumes. This book I have found in very few libraries since. It contains a very concise history of the Jewish nation and a comprehensive account of the events leading up to the fall of Jerusalem and its capture by the Romans. Among other books I remember Fox's *Book of Martyrs*, in a number of volumes, Bunyan's *Pilgrims Progress*, and *Holy War*, Nieburgh's history of Rome, one of the most comprehensive histories that has ever been written, and one of the driest.

I do not know how a boy of fourteen ever waded through and mastered it. No doubt a great inclination to acquire knowledge and the fact that I had never seen or heard of any lighter literature helped me very much. A little later on a friend let me have the five volumes of Macaulay's *History of England*, which had just been published in this country. I was so taken with the beautiful language and the grand roll of its sentences that I could hardly take time to eat or sleep. I was just recovering from a fever and lay in bed and, as I was very weak, I remember the doctor ordered my books taken from me, and only given back so many hours a day.

My time was not, however, all taken up with work and reading. Saturday afternoons, unless very busy, were given over to hunting, fishing or swimming when it was warm enough. I had an old revolutionary flint-lock musket that would shoot about as hard backward as forward. But, as I have before said, I never became a great hunter. I loved better to sit in the shade on the river bank with my line in the stream, and oblivious of all around me dream the dreams of boyhood. I think I was rather disappointed than otherwise when a nibble would recall me to this every-day world. I don't remember, however, of its ever going beyond a nibble.

A few times, however, I enjoyed a hunt. Once I remember I had been plowing in a small rented field a mile from home, and had worked until dusk, when I unhitched and, mounting one of the horses, started for home along a road through the woods. I had only gone about half way when I heard a loud flapping of wings on my right and, looking up toward an immense oak on the summit of a hill, I beheld silhouetted against the sky the largest wild turkey I had ever seen, standing erect on a large branch that overtopped the other trees. I took a careful survey of the surroundings and when I arrived home, had unharnessed and fed the horses, I found my supper ready. As soon as I had satisfied my wants, my father with his Kentucky rifle and I with the old flint-lock musket started back. The moon was just rising as we neared the place, and in silence I piloted the way to a place in the vicinity of the tree and from where we could see in the dim light Mr. Gobbler quietly resting. My father fired with his rifle and missed. The old bird straightened up on his perch and my father, dropping his rifle, grabbed the musket from my hands and fired again. The turkey came tumbling down and had no sooner reached the ground than I was on him. It was lucky that I had hurried for but one of the shots had struck him and he was only stunned.

I grabbed him by the neck and tried to hold him down, but in a moment he was from under me and was drawing the blood from my hands with his sharp claws. I thought surely he would beat me out, but I kept on twisting his neck until finally I shut off his wind. He certainly was the largest turkey, wild or tame, I have ever seen.

Speaking of the old musket recalls a story. We were greatly annoyed by an immense half wild hog that would break our fences and destroy the growing corn. One evening about dusk the baying of the dogs told us that the hog was again at his mischief. My father in his wrath seized the old flint-lock and, ramming home a dozen buck shot on top of the bird shot, crossed over to the field. He saw the old porker standing at bay, surrounded by the dogs, and, slipping up to the fence, took aim and fired. The musket went off and so did the hog, the gun flying out of my father's hands and over the fence into the weeds and undergrowth, and in passing cut a severe gash in his cheek. I remember his returning to the house with the blood running down his face. He had not stopped to look for the gun and it was forgotten. The next day a neighbor came bringing it in. He said that in passing along the fence he saw a great commotion in the weeds and, climbing over to investigate, he saw the old gun among the brush, still kicking for all it was worth, and he had to use all his strength and skill to subdue it. As this is intended to be a veracious chronicle, I do not vouch for this story, but give it to you just as it was told. It is a matter of absolute knowledge to me that the old gun could kick some.

With the cool weather in October and November we were always out at daylight and down to the pasture in a race with the hogs for the hickory nuts, which had fallen during the night. We used to gather barrels of them and of the old black walnuts, and lay them by for the long winter evenings.

I had continued my studies whenever possible, and by the time I had reached my sixteenth year I had mastered arithmetic, geography and English grammar, as far as was taught in our schools.

One day in March, 1852, my father came out to the field where I was plowing for the corn planting and said that I had worked so faithfully for so many years and that my brothers were now large enough to take my place, that I had gone as far in school as the teachers could take me, and that my grandfather in Kentucky wanted me to come and stay a year with him and attend the academy there.

This seemed as though some of my dreams were to come

true. It was so much beyond my fondest anticipations that I could not express my gratitude.

The next week was a busy one of preparation. Some friends were going within a few miles of my destination, and I was placed in their care. As the time drew near for my departure the thought of leaving father and mother, brothers and sisters became such a nightmare to me that I would have gone back to the plow if I had dared, and my pride would have permitted me.

At that time a journey of five hundred miles was like going out of the world. On the appointed day, with a heavy heart I bade farewell to all the family but my father, who went with me to Hannibal. The fine steamboat "Fashion" lay at the wharf. Leaving the land for the first time in my life, I went on board and in a few minutes the ropes were cast off and we launched out on the bosom of the great "Father of Waters."

One cannot describe the awe and the heavy heart that a diffident, awkward, backwoods boy can feel when for the first time he is thrown among strangers and in surroundings before unknown.

The boat was crowded and there was room at the tables for not more than one-third of the passengers. I could not crowd, and consequently always found myself at the third table, and what was left by that time was not enough to hurt, nor was it fit for anyone to eat. There were no sleeping berths for even the women, and the men were given a pair of blankets and the liberty to choose their own sleeping apartment. I found the best place under the tables in the main cabin, for there you were not in danger of being walked over every few minutes. The only trouble was that the tables were not cleared until very late, and were re-set about daylight.

I do not remember that those inconveniences annoyed me very much. I was so taken up with the strange scenes, the changing shores, and a thousand other things new to me that it seemed immaterial whether I ate or slept.

Thus we went down the river, stopping at various towns until we reached St. Louis. Here we were transferred to a smaller and less crowded boat, bound for Louisville, Kentucky. As this boat started at once I had no opportunity to see the city of St. Louis.

From a short distance below St. Louis to the mouth of the Ohio the banks of the Mississippi on the Missouri side are very precipitous. At St. Genevieve and other places were shot towers built on an overhanging cliff, the shot falling to the level of the river.

I do not think I slept much on this journey. I was up on the "hurricane deck" early of a morning and until late at night, watching the changing scenes on either bank.

We landed at every little town to take on or put off passengers and freight. It was wonderful to watch the deck hands work. While the boat was running they lay around on the lower deck, playing cards, singing to the accompaniment of a banjo or sleeping in the sun. But when a landing was made and the mate appeared, every man-jack of them was galvanized into new life, and things moved faster than I ever saw them before or after. It was necessary for a mate to know how to rule men, and to be a past master of the language of the river. The mighty oaths he swore were enough to burn holes in the floor or to turn the air blue.

The deck hands had to be on call at all hours of the day or night. Sometimes I have sat on the upper deck at almost midnight, looking out on what seemed a virgin forest, down to the river's edge. Suddenly the steamer would give a peculiar whistle, lights would appear on the bank of the river, the boat would round to and tie up to a stump and all hands would leap ashore where the wood was piled. It was surprising how quickly fifty or sixty cords could be carried aboard and piled up conveniently for the firemen to feed into the furnace.

At Cairo we turned into the Ohio, and, instead of going with the current, we had to breast the waters, so our advance became much slower.

On the sixth day we reached Louisville, where we left the boat and boarded the first railroad train I had ever seen, for Lexington. The route was through Frankfort, the Capital of the State, arriving at Lexington at noon. From here we traveled by stage to Paris, some ten miles.

At Paris I parted from my traveling companions and, hiring a saddle horse, arrived at Cynthiana after dark, where I inquired the road to my grandfather's place, whose home was two miles beyond the town. The clerk at the hotel advised me to remain over night. He said the road was very hard to find, the night being dark, and I could never find the way. With my usual pertinacity I declined to stay, as I had made up my mind to sleep that night in my grandfather's house. The hotel clerk gave me very elaborate directions, which I followed for half a mile, then became helplessly lost. I wandered on for several miles, and then retraced my steps, intending to go to the hotel. Just as I reached the outskirts of the town I met half a dozen Negroes, who had been in town on a lark. I stopped them and when I finally persuaded them to talk I found that one of the young fellows belonged to a near neighbor of my grandfather, so they feared I might inform on them. When I promised to keep "mum," the young man mounted behind me and in an hour I arrived at my destination.

CHAPTER FIVE

REMEMBRANCES OF SCHOOL-DAYS AND KENTUCKY HOMES

I FOUND MY SURROUNDINGS so different on arriving at my grandfather's house, from any I had ever known, that for a time I could not fully comprehend the change. From Frankfort to Lexington and on to Cynthiana seemed like one beautiful park. Fields of hundreds and thousands of acres covered with a growth of most verdant blue-grass, with here and there scattered clumps of hickory, beech and sugar maple and other trees of magnificent proportions. Over these fields roamed herds of thoroughbred horses and cattle.

The houses were solidly built either of brick or stone, which to me appeared veritable palaces. The fences, instead of being built of "split rails," were all of limestone. You could ride all day between those stone fences, built to last a thousand years. The roads were all turnpikes, that is a road thrown up round and then covered thickly with broken rock. Such roads would last with little repairs for hundreds of years. At this time they were all toll roads, that is, people who had money would join together and procure from the court a franchise to build and maintain a road between certain points for a number of years. In consideration of keeping such roads in repair, they were permitted to erect toll gates at certain distances apart and to collect toll in the amount fixed by the court. You could not travel in any direction without coming to one of these gates, where you had to pay before it was opened. Foot passengers went free, horseback five cents, single buggy ten cents and double buggy or two-horse wagon twenty-five cents, and so on. However, it was pleasant to travel on such beautiful roads. But there have been no toll gates there for years. The roads were gradually bought by the county, the gates taken down and the care for repairs became a county tax.

Looking backward it seems to me that the old blue-grass country was in every way the most beautiful in the world, and I have never since been so impressed by any other land. I would be glad to have the reader see it as it appeared to me. But any language I have seems so inadequate to express my feelings that I could not do it justice. I have preserved a copy of a poem, which I read at the time, and which appears to me to so perfectly describe many homes that I knew, that it seems not inappropriate to introduce it here.

> I know a house, its open doors
>   Wide set to catch the scented breeze;
> While dimpling all the oaken floors,
>   Faint shadows of the swaying trees
> Pass in and out, like spectral things—
>   Dim creatures born of summer light;
> Till through the deepening twilight springs
>   A paler radiance of light.
>
> Then softly in those silent hours
>   Fair faces grow upon the gloom,
> And whisper'd words of unseen powers
>   Breathe inward with the garden bloom
> Of roses clinging to the walls,
>   And lawns smooth mown with punctual shears,
> While over roof and threshold falls
>   The peace of many a hundred years.
>
> Unfolding slow their ivory fringe,
>   The lilies lie upon the pond;
> The firs have caught the sunset tinge,
>   And murmur elfin-like beyond.
> I think whoever sought that grove
>   To dream an hour of love or heaven
> Might, wrapt in some strange mystery, rove
>   And find his years had grown to seven.

Great elms, a glorious altar veil
   Screen off the yellow evening skies,
'Mid those thick branches blue and pale,
   The Genii smoke doth curling rise,
And, wavering in the waveless air,
   A certain tender touch impart
To what where else too calmly fair,
   Like memory in some heaven-taught heart.

Across the broad unbroken glade
   Which girds this house on either hand,
The beech clumps sprinkle showers of shade,
   These outposts of the forests stand
And guard the kingdom of the deer;
   The stillness of their charmed domain,
Where Spring chimes Matins every year,
   And Autumn leaves fall like rain.

For miles those beeches rise and fall,
   And ripple like some inland sea;
From bough to bough the wild birds call
   And squirrels nest on every tree;
Blue depths of distance melt away
   As far as vision may discern,
And all the open slopes are gay
   With fox glove and the tangled fern.

Such are some of my remembrances of an old Kentucky home. To me it was an entire change of environment, and it seems to me that it was only a short time before I was able to adapt myself to the change. Instead of rising with the approach of light, clothing myself in homespun and working hard all day, with only such stray moments as I could snatch for study, and only the good but backwoods young people for associates, I found myself suddenly clothed in comfortable, well-made, if plain, garments. I did not have to arise until the sun was up, and I could sit and study in my room as late as I pleased.

Cynthiana is among the oldest settlements in Kentucky. The older people, if not highly educated, were well bred and cultured. Really poor people were almost unknown. All were natives of the United States, mostly of old Virginia, Maryland or Carolina stock. At that time I only remember one person of foreign birth, a little son of Abraham, who owned a clothing store.

It was strenuously cultivated into the minds of old and young to be courteous and never to give offense, but they were quick to resent even the appearance of an affront, hence the people were always on guard, and a more polite, hospitable people it has never been my pleasure to meet. The boys and girls were in many ways superior to those I had before known and when I started to the academy, I was treated with the greatest consideration by nearly everyone. Though I felt like a backward boy, I was soon placed at my ease, and it was but a short time until I felt like one of them.

I was somewhat of an athlete along certain lines and attained a good standing among those of my own age. I believe on the hundred-yard dash and in the standing and running broad jump I held the record in the academy.

I soon found it paid to be courteous and also that I might have to fight to retain the respect of my companions. In my class there was a young man, who befriended me in various ways, who kept me out of trouble, stood by me on all occasions and gave me his open friendship.

There was another young fellow about a year older than I, the son of a distiller, who was one of the few dissipated young men I remember. He was also a bully. From the first he seemed to dislike me, and never let an opportunity pass to be offensive. My friend took me aside one day and said: "That young man will destroy your good standing in the class if let alone. The next time he uses insulting language I am going to give him a thrashing." I told him I appreciated his friendship, and that I was satisfied he was right, but that I had decided from the start to fight my own battles. He called my attention to the fact that the fellow was older, larger and stronger than I—at the same time advised me to go ahead.

The very next time he used insulting language I struck

him in the face with my open hand. The boys gathered around and, as fighting was not allowed on the school grounds, it was arranged that we should meet in a certain grove the next Saturday and fight it out. I am free to acknowledge that I was nearly scared to death, but fully realized that my future in the school depended on my standing by my guns. One thing encouraged me very much. Nearly all the boys were my friends and I knew I would have fair play. Several of the boys took me in hand and gave me some elementary lessons in boxing. On Saturday we met. When the argument began I soon found that I was his superior in activity, and if I could keep away from a clinch I had a chance. But somehow he got hold of me, threw me and began to pummel me in good shape. I knew I was "all in" and bawled enough, and they separated us. By this time I was good and mad, and told him among other things that I would fight him every Saturday as long as I lived. The next Saturday's story was about the same. I was whipped again.

In the meantime my instructors were busy in giving me lessons in the manly art of self-defense, and the third Saturday I was full of confidence. I kept the bully off beautifully, in the meantime battering his ribs until he was very tired, and at last, somehow, I reached the point of his chin and he was down and out for good. He was so long in recovering consciousness that I was scared worse than ever.

I had established my reputation for grit, and I never had the least trouble as long as I remained in Kentucky. If they had only known how repugnant the whole thing was to me and that only my pride kept me up to the mark, I should never have had the reputation I enjoyed, but did not deserve.

CHAPTER SIX

AN EVENTFUL RETURN TRIP TO THE MISSOURI FARM

But I must get back to my story. I spent a couple of days in rest, then a friend took me to the academy, a two-story brick building most beautifully situated on a hill, commanding a view of the whole town. I was introduced to Mr. W. W. Crutchfield, the principal, a man of perhaps fifty years, and a graduate of the University of Virginia.

He was the finest scholar in Latin and Greek I have ever known, and also well versed in all branches of learning usually taught at that day, except perhaps the higher mathematics. I do not remember a single pupil in the school pursuing these studies. This suited me entirely, as I never had any desire for the higher mathematics, but a great and abiding love for languages and literature.

Mr. Crutchfield put me through a pretty stiff examination in reading, geography and English grammar. I was very much gratified and very agreeably surprised with his report. I was put to work immediately in the study of Latin, natural and mental philosophy, with an hour or two a day in the higher English branches. I was happy in my surroundings and studied hard not only during school hours but at home also, and, as I had but few places to visit, my holidays were spent in special studies.

When vacation arrived in May, 1853, I found the funds that I had taken with me about exhausted. My grandfather did not seem to understand that I might need money and I was far too proud to ask for it. I knew my father had his hands full caring for the younger members of our family, and, while I knew he would help me, I could not for a moment think of calling on him for any assistance.

I had received a full year of schooling and determined to return home and earn money for further study. I knew if I wrote home informing my family of my determination I would be ordered to remain where I was, and that money would be sent to keep me another year. Therefore I kept my intention entirely to myself until the last day of school.

I told my grandfather that as there was such a long vacation (some three months) I wished to go home, to which he readily consented. I had barely enough money to pay my way, if everything went well. During the year my parents had sold the farm and purchased a new one on the Meramec River, in Crawford County, two hundred miles south of our old home, and to me a *terra incognita*. I searched the map carefully and concluded that a town on the Mississippi River called Herculaneum would land me nearer home than any other point, so, packing my books and clothing in an old carpet bag, a friend took me in his buggy to a town eighteen miles distant, from which place there was a stage to Cincinnati. There was no public conveyance from Cynthiana or Paris or even Lexington. The freight was all hauled by teams and the few people who traveled went in their own conveyances, family carriages or on horseback. I think the place where I took the stage was called Leesburg, and I arrived in Cincinnati toward evening.

On inquiry I found that the regular passenger steamboat had gone the day before. The state of my finance forbidding my waiting for the next boat, I engaged passage on a freighter, which also carried a few passengers, about the only difference being that the freight boat was slower and stopped at every landing to take on or put off freight. However, I had all summer before me and as the boat furnished meals to passengers, it was cheaper, a considerable recommendation to me at that time. The slow trip down the Ohio to Cairo and up the Mississippi was full of interest.

On the eighth day, just after the noon meal, I was informed that we were approaching Herculaneum. I got my old carpet bag out and descended to the lower deck. On looking around I could see no town or wharf, only a shot tower on an overhanging bluff, and a low point of land jutting out into the river. The boat made for this low point, and without tying up or entirely stopping, a gang plank was run out and I was hustled ashore, while the boat kept right on up the river. On looking at my surroundings, not a soul was in sight. On one side of me flowed the river, and on the other side of the spit of land on which I stood was a slough some hundred yards wide and apparently very deep. At the head of the point was a perpendicular bluff several hundred feet high. I was as effectually marooned as though I were on an island in the middle of the ocean.

I sat down to consider the situation and if there was a possible way out. On the other side of the slough and under the bluff I observed several boats tied to the bank. I finally concluded that I could safely swim the hundred yards, borrow a boat, row back for my clothes and bag, and then somehow make my way up the bluff. I had just commenced stripping for the swim when a young man hailed me from the top of the cliff and when I had explained the situation, he said for me to wait and that he would come down and row me over. In a short time he appeared. Loosening one of the boats he rowed over, and took me across. I found that there was a trail which I could not see from the other side, winding up to the top of the cliff. A few hundred yards back was a fine low-roofed old Southern house, which was the home of the young man. He took me in with him and introduced me to his father and mother, a married sister, and her two children. I was received with the old-time Southern hospitality and made to feel at home, as I seldom have felt in a strange family. They inquired who I was, where I was going, and expressed by their actions an interest in me that was pleasant indeed. They told me it was fortunate that they had seen the boat, as one seldom landed there any more and there was no possible way from the landing, except by crossing the slough. However, I had an idea that I would have "found a way." I am sure I could have negotiated the swim, stolen a boat and gotten across. These people treated me as one of the family. We had an old-fashioned Southern Sunday dinner, (I believe I have not told the reader it was Sunday I landed), fried chicken, corn bread and all the good things the old Negro cook knew so well how to prepare.

The stage from St. Louis to Patosi passed on the road a quarter of a mile distant, at eleven o'clock the next morning, which would take me by evening to a small town about twenty miles from my home; so after a good breakfast, when the hour for the stage to pass had arrived, the whole family accompanied me to the road. They would not accept a cent for their hospitality and all they had done for me, but the reader may rest assured that I left my heartfelt thanks with this good, old, aristocratic family. It is sad to think that there are not many of their kind left in the world. It seems to me at this writing that all my life I have been fortunate enough always to find friends when in need. I do not know why it was. The only reason I can imagine is that I was always open and frank, and told the whole truth. Strangers never seemed to doubt me, and I have been led to conclude that nothing will carry one so far as an open, manly course of action.

Towards evening we reached the little mining hamlet to which I had been directed. There was a small hotel at which I remained over night. The next morning I was told that no conveyance could be had in the direction I wished to go, but at a store and post office called Fourch Arno, seven miles on my way, I would probably find teams from the Meramec that would take me near my home.

Bright and early I shouldered my bag, which, beside my clothing, contained all my books, and must have weighed fifty pounds. However, I started out and about ten o'clock a.m. reached the store. The owner said he knew my father very well as he came there (eighteen miles from his home) for supplies. He said he would gladly loan me his saddle horse, but his brother had taken it out and he did not know if he would be home before night. He added that if I would remain as his guest over night I could have the horse and welcome. I was so anxious to reach home that I did not feel like considering his kind proposition. I thanked him, and as two men were there with an ox team going twelve miles on my way, they offered me conveyance as far as they went. My bag was placed on the wagon. They asked me to ride, but as they both walked, I was too proud to accept, and preferred to walk with them. The way lay across a long pine ridge, with a gravelly soil, and the oxen were very slow. The day was warm, my feet were becoming blistered, but I kept up a bold front. At least I was getting along faster than if I was carrying my heavy bag.

When we arrived at the place where they turned off, I bade them good-bye, again shouldered my pack, and trudged on. I now commenced passing cabins of the settlers every few miles, as the soil became better, and when I stopped to inquire if I was on the right road, the good women would ask me in to rest a while, and bring me bread and fresh milk, which refreshed me for another effort.

I came next to a beautiful, clear stream, which I learned later was called Fourch Basil. (This country was settled first by the French, and the streams all had French names as "Fourch Arno," "Fourch Renault," "Fourch Basil," and so on. The word "Fourch" in French, I understand, has the same meaning as branch or creek.) I took off my shoes and socks and waded Fourch Basil, bathed my blistered feet in the clear, cold water, lay down on the bank and drank deeply, and felt better. A little farther on I stopped at a better house, with nice fields of young corn and wheat, in the creek bottoms. The people here were as kindly and hospitable as all the others, so I had my regular milk and was told that it was less than two miles to my destination, but these two miles were the longest I ever traveled. I was so thoroughly exhausted that I could only go a hundred or two yards until I would have to drop my pack and lie down by the roadside for a short time to rest. At last, just as the sun was sinking in the West, my home came in sight. None too soon, as I had walked twenty-five miles, the greater part of the way carrying fully fifty pounds.

I took the family by surprise, as they supposed I was back in Kentucky. Nevertheless I was received with open arms, and in a day or two, with a good constitution and youth, I had forgotten all my weariness.

CHAPTER SEVEN

SCHOOL TEACHING AND GOOD TIMES ON THE MERAMEC RIVER

I FOUND THE SCHOOL, about a mile from my father's house, without a teacher. The trustees offered me the position, which I accepted, immediately went to Steeleville, the County Seat, and took the examination from the County Superintendent of Schools, passing it successfully, and in two weeks from the time I arrived at home I was installed in the school, being only a few months over seventeen years old.

I will anticipate to say here that I taught this school successfully for three terms of three months each, there being three terms in a year.

I found our new home a very comfortable one, a frame house rather superior to any in that portion of the country. It was built by a pioneer of the West in 1824. The lumber was all "whip sawed," that is, sawed by hand. It was said to have been the first frame house built in all that part of the country. One of my sons recently visited the old home and he reports the house still standing and in a good state of preservation.

The farm of some four hundred acres was situated on the Meramec River, one of the most beautiful streams I have ever seen anywhere. Its head waters were only forty miles above, and it came from the earth, not a little rivulet, but one immense spring covering more than an acre, from which the stream flowed to the depth of three feet and more than fifty yards wide. Where we lived it had been increased by numerous smaller streams flowing into it to a hundred yards wide and a depth in many places of fifteen to twenty feet, while every few miles there were riffles where it could be forded on horseback or in wagon at low or even ordinary stage of water. Except after heavy rains, the stream was perfectly clear, and one could see the bottom almost anywhere. One of the favorite amusements was fishing with a long-handled spear from a dugout or canoe.

I had not been teaching long before I caught the canoe fever badly, and (I had an expert to work at once) a magnificent ash was felled and a piece sawed off twenty feet long. This was hewn off on the side intended for the bottom until there was a flat surface of two and one-half feet. The opposite side was then dug out, leaving walls and bottom of about two inches in thickness. When finished the canoe was twenty feet long, two and a half feet broad, and sixteen inches high. The bow was rounded off in such a manner as to insure the least resistance to the water. The stern was shaped with a seat for the person who used the single paddle with which it was propelled. Such a canoe was very strong and very light, when without a load almost sitting on the water, and with from four to six persons in it floating in four inches, and with its broad bottom it could hardly be overturned. I soon became an expert oarsman, and during the summer spent most of my idle time on the river. On a Saturday I would paddle miles up the rapid current, often resting by the way, then I would lie down, with my head on the seat, and let the canoe float down while I would dream dreams, beautiful and bright dreams that alas! never came entirely true in this world. Sometimes I would work my way above certain rapids, where years before, a kind of dam had been made across the stream for a fish trap. Here the current was very swift, and jagged rocks showed their heads through the spray, and it was glorious fun to steer the canoe at racing speed through the rocks and foam into the calm water below. Again I would stand in the bow of the boat, with spear in hand, ready to strike at any fish I could see passing in the waters below. Some varieties of fish are very easily speared, being slow in their movements, while others, like the black bass, are almost impossible to take this way. When the winter came on the water was much clearer, and when it was very cold the fish would gather in the deepest holes until they covered the bottom of the river.

I remember one cold day when the thermometer was almost zero, that one of my big school boys and I floated down to the deepest place in the river, where the water was nearly twenty feet deep, and loaded the canoe with all we wanted of great big ten to twenty-pound fish, all in a few hours. It was so cold that every time we let the spear with its long handle down, when it was pulled up the water would freeze, and it would soon become so unwieldy that we would have to stop and knock the ice off before we could continue.

The Meramec River, coming from springs, and having a very strong current, never froze over, though ice often formed in eddies and along the banks. The country around the Meramec is the most picturesque of any that I remember. It is largely a mineral-producing country, large amounts of lead ore was produced for many miles around, and some very rich iron mines were in the vicinity. The country is almost mountainous, the river in many places being buttressed by frowning cliffs many hundred feet high. Along the river and its tributaries are very rich alluvial bottoms on which corn and all kinds of farm and garden products grow in abundance. The lands back from these consist first of bench lands, which are fairly productive, and back of these is the "forest primeval," extending for miles over a hilly, almost mountainous, country. I remember one round hill near where I taught, overlooking all the surrounding country. It was heavily timbered half way up, and then for half a mile to the summit not a sign of vegetation. Nothing but loose red earth in which one would sink over their shoe tops, making climbing very difficult. On my last visit an iron furnace had been erected, and this loose red earth was being shoveled up and made into the finest iron. It was simply iron ore which had been oxidized by exposure to the atmosphere for ages. Under it was a solid mountain of iron.

I finished the school year of nine months in March, and could have stayed longer but I had saved enough money from my princely salary of twenty-five dollars a month to return to my studies and complete my academic course. The only incident of the winter that comes vividly to my mind is that my father, sometime in the fall, being in St. Louis, bought himself a beautiful fur cap, the finest I had ever seen, the softest fur and a large band of the same material around it, that could be turned down at will, sheltering the ears and throat. I wanted that cap very much, would have given him an advance on its original cost, five dollars, but he would not talk about it; I kept up my importunity and finally he said as he had a good deal of fencing to do, if I would split out one thousand rails at the usual price of fifty cents per hundred, I could have the cap. I have no doubt he intended to bluff me, as one hundred rails was a good day's work for a man used to the work. However, I called his bluff, and the next morning with ax, maul and iron wedges I started at daylight. There was a piece of fine oak timber on the road to the school house, and every morning I worked until school time and after school until dark, and all day Saturday. In less time than one would think, my task was completed and I sported that fur cap for a good many winters afterwards. My! though it was a task. The first hour I blistered my hands and all the time I was at it the snow was from six inches to a foot deep, but I want my descendants to know that Lincoln was not the only rail splitter.

CHAPTER EIGHT

DECISION TO ADOPT LITERATURE AS A PROFESSION

I RETURNED TO CYNTHIANA and to my studies in the spring of 1854, nothing new in my journey occurred, the only difference being that a railroad had been opened from Cincinnati as far as Cynthiana. During the year of my absence I had put in a good many hours on Latin, and Greek, and Philosophy, both natural and moral, and I was surprised that I was soon able to take my place in my classes. During this year I must have studied very hard, as I not only kept my standing in my classes, but got through a good deal of miscellaneous reading. My greatest delight was in the Latin, and during school I read the required number of books in Caesar, Virgil, Cicero and the other text books, but I had become so interested in the stories that during the long summer vacation I read the remainder of Caesar's Commentaries, completed the Eneid, and many of Cicero's orations. During this year I had taken greatly to literature, read all the poets I could get hold of, and concluded to adopt it as a profession.

Of course, being only eighteen years old, my first attempts were in verse. At that time there a paper published in Louisville whose editor was a poet of distinction, and was a great friend of the young. I wrote considerably for publication, and now I think at the age of seventy-six that my poems were not entirely bad; that if I had possessed the means to continue along this line I might in the end have met with some measure of success. I do not wish my readers to take my judgment on this point, and think it will not be inappropriate to introduce two or three short poems at this time, not that I think they will compare with the writings of the great ones of the earth, but I wish my children, grandchildren and their descendants to know as far as I can portray it, every phase of my life and character. It seems to me a psychological problem why boys (I believe girls, too) who try to write, always begin with death and the grave, and the hereafter. But I think it is true, and I was no exception to the rule, my first published writing was entitled:

WHEN I MUST SLEEP

When I must sleep low in the tomb,
    As sleep at last I must,
I ask no stone with sculptured base
    To mark my lifeless dust.

But I would have some forest tree
    Spread its broad arms above,
Where little birds might come and sing
    Their symphonies of love.

I would not have the willow tree
    Stand drooping o'er my grave,
Nor should the funeral cypress there
    Its gloomy foliage wave.

Let Nature there her carpet spread,
    And brightest flowers bloom;
Let violets and roses spread
    Their fragrance and perfume.

A little later on I published a poem entitled "The Home of Stella May," a portion of which reads as follows:

Where first is heard the wild bird's song,
The sweet Meander flows along,

Its soft and mossy banks between.
Sometimes it glides through meadows green,
Then softly murmurs through the grove,
Singing songs of quiet love.

And then with quick and sudden bound,
That echoes through the woods around,
The streamlet wakes to life again
And rushes through the darkening glen.
Here hanging o'er the crystal stream,
Far brighter than a poet's dream
And fair as bloom in peri's bowers,
Blush the wildwood's loveliest flowers.

'Tis here the hawthorne rears its head,
While o'er the stream its branches spread.
'Tis here the rose and violet bloom,
And here the sweetbriar's rich perfume
Is spread upon the air,
Or hanging o'er the stream so bright,
They see by morning's rosy light
Each floweret mirrored there.

And yonder on that rising ground,
By hoary oaks and maples crowned,
And where yon elm tree rises high
Its head toward the deep blue sky.
'Tis there within that sylvan shade

DECISION TO ADOPT LITERATURE AS A PROFESSION

Which Nature's own great love has made;
'Tis there, where earliest falls the dew,
Where shrubs and flowers hide from view,
Where shade and sunshine mingling play—
There is the home of Stella May.

Stella May was a cousin of mine, though that was not her real name, and she lived in a beautiful spot. Perhaps poetic license has made it more beautiful than the real.

I will only give one other of a different meter and written shortly before returning to Missouri. I must have been very blue when I wrote it, but then if people of imagination were not sometimes blue there would be no real verse.

MEMORIA IN ETERNA

Again, my rude harp, I will wake thy wild numbers
To sing of the pleasures and friends that were mine,
And when it is finished, away to thy slumbers—
'Tis the last wreath of song we ever may twine.

I had dreamed that thy notes ne'er again would be heard;
That thy cords were all broken, thy music all hushed
On the rough sea of life, in the battle and strife
The bright dreams that awoke thee too rudely were crushed.

But the days long departed again come around me,

And scenes that from memory can never depart;
The hopes that I cherished, the friends that I loved,
Though I see them no more, are engraved on my heart.

And thou Licking again I can see thee roll by,
And I know 'tis not fancy or the poet's wild dream
That has made thee appear so surpassingly lovely
And as pure and as clear as Chindara—sweet stream.

 I remember the meadows, the fields and the grove
Where I wandered with friends or else sat 'neath the bowers
Which Nature had formed, our hearts bounding with love,
We would crown some fair brow with a chaplet of flowers.

But alas! They are past, and forever are gone,
Are those days with the hopes, which so freely they gave.
Disappointment forever soon darkened them all,
And together they vanished beneath Time's murky wave.

Yet the Licking rolls on and the flowers still bloom,
And the voice of the young is still heard in the grove,
While a wanderer far, I disconsolate roam
From the friends of my youth and the place that I love.

Then farewell to the scenes and the friends of the past;
Though no more I may greet you, this rude verse of mine,
A tribute that comes from the heart pure and holy,
I bring and lay down at fond memory's shrine.

CHAPTER NINE

STUDY OF MEDICINE WHILE ENGAGED IN TEACHING

TO RETURN TO MY NARRATIVE, I finished the course in the academy in December, 1855, and at once took cars for Cincinnati, and a boat from there to St. Louis. I remember nothing particular of this trip except that the day or two before we reached St. Louis the weather became very cold and before we arrived there the river was full of running ice. The boat made but little headway and it was doubtful if we would be able to reach our destination; however, we arrived late in the evening of December twenty-second. On the next morning the Mississippi was frozen entirely over, and the boat could go no further. Many passengers for farther up the river were unable to reach their homes. A boy about my own age had paid all the money he had for his fare on the boat to a point some hundred miles up the river. I took him to my room for the night and the next morning I gave him five dollars, just half of all I had. I never heard from him again, but, no doubt he reached home, as he had but little farther to go.

The next day was so cold and snowing that the trains were not running. On the morning of the twenty-fourth I took the train to Pacific, forty miles, this being as far as the road was built at that time. I arrived at Pacific about noon, had lunch, and shouldering my valise, struck out for home, forty miles distant. That afternoon I made twenty miles before dark, though the roads were heavy with snow, which had not yet been packed to any extent by the travel. I stayed over night with some people whom I knew when I was at home before, and after a good night's rest and an early, but hearty breakfast, on Christmas morning I was off at the break of day, and arrived at home just as they were sitting down to their Christmas dinner. With my welcome home and a good dinner, and a night's rest, I felt no bad effects from my long walk. Although it was broken by a night's rest, I had walked over forty miles in about ten hours over almost impassable roads.

Of course, I wanted to be doing something, and though I would not follow teaching as a profession, it looked like the only thing for me to do, until I saw an opening to enter into some more profitable business. The schools in the county were all provided with teachers, it being in the middle of the term, but there was one unorganized district some six miles across the Meramec where there was a good schoolhouse and some thirty-five children, large boys and girls, wanting a teacher. The parents subscribed a certain number of pupils and paid one dollar per month for each, so that a teacher, if he collected closely, could make thirty-five dollars per month, instead of the regular price in the public schools of twenty-five.

There were a number of big, rowdy boys in this school from sixteen to eighteen, who had made life unendurable for teachers for the last few years. They would lock the door and keep the teacher and pupils out. They had waylayed the teachers and beaten them up and, of course, had grown bolder each year. I hesitated a long time before I would tackle the proposition, but as I could find nothing else to do I finally accepted the position. I figured that if I was to teach the term out I must not allow these boys to get together before I proved my authority. I felt myself good for any one of them, but in the past they had piled a half dozen on the teacher at once. I opened school on Monday morning and all went well for the first few days, but towards the end of the week it was evident something was going on. The second Monday I walked in ostentatiously, displaying a big, black hickory, and put it carefully by my desk. I had my mind made up to look for trouble. The largest boy, and ringleader, sat near me on the left. About an hour after school opened I ordered the advanced pupils to spend a half hour in writing. As soon as they were well under way I called the bully's attention to the fact that he was holding his pen incorrectly and that he must correct it. I made my voice as imperative and offensive as possible. He answered back that he would hold his pen as he pleased. Seizing my hickory in my right hand I was on him in an instant, and as he was leaning over the desk, before he could think, I had him by his coat collar, pulled him over the top of his desk, landing him face down on the floor. He kicked and squirmed, and swore, but I held him safe. All the time the hickory was raising stripes on his back and legs. I gave him a good thrashing and kept on until he promised to behave. I let him up, and told him to go home. He did not return for several days, and I heard, through some of the children, that he was having his wounds dressed and was unable to sit down. When he returned he came to me in a manly way and said he had concluded that I could run the school, and that if any further trouble came up I could count on him. He remained a good friend, and I never taught a better school.

In this connection I want to say that I have always avoided trouble whenever possible, but if I see it coming, and unavoidable, I have found it best to meet it a little more than half way. I taught this school until the summer vacation, but as it was a great deal of work to collect my money, I concluded to look in another direction.

STUDY OF MEDICINE WHILE ENGAGED IN TEACHING

In the meantime, an educated man in St. Louis, Rev. R. A. Young, whom I had met and who had taken an interest in me, asked me to visit him while in St. Louis. During the vacation I visited some relatives in that city and called on him. In our talk the choice of a profession came up and he thought I should take up the study of medicine, even if I never practiced, and following his advice I visited Dr. Polk, the Dean of the St. Louis Medical College, who kindly made me out a list of books that I could study, between times, while teaching. I carried those books home with me and for a year I put in every spare hour on them. While in St. Louis I saw an ad in a paper for a teacher, offering one hundred dollars per quarter of the twelve weeks, for one qualified for the position at Mount Sterling, Mo. This was a larger salary than I had ever received, or known of anyone receiving. I applied for the school, and my offer was accepted. In looking it up I found Mount Sterling was about fifty miles from my home on the Gasconade River. There was a cross-country mail route from Potosi to Mount Sterling, the mail being carried by a boy on horseback. I managed to load my books and some clothing on a young horse I had raised and got the boy to take the balance. That afternoon we went across the most bushy and unsettled country I had ever seen, and stayed over night at a Mr. Burchard's, who owned a fine farm on a small stream called the Borbois. The next day we traveled over some prairie and more broken country, arriving about two p.m. at a Mr. Cooper's, who was one of the Trustees of the school, and with whom I had engaged board. This Mr. Cooper was Sheriff of the county, with a wife and four nearly grown children. I found the town of Mount Sterling most beautifully situated on the banks of the Gasconade River. There were quite a number of houses, but not a single inhabitant, and the buildings looked as though they had not been occupied for years. I never learned the cause of this "deserted village" with its beautiful situation on the bank of as fine a stream as there is in the world. The Gasconade River heads up in the Ozark Mountains and debouches into the Missouri River at a point about fifteen miles north of Mount Sterling. At the latter place it is a stream of some six hundred feet in width, with clear water, and quite deep. On the banks are fine alluvial bottom, owned by a few wealthy people who were slaveholders. I found that the county as far as the Missouri River was rolling hills and occupied entirely by Germans, who had come over in colonies, bringing their customs, language, wooden shoes, preachers and teachers with them. The principal town was Herman, the county seat—all Germans. In the school district where I was to teach I found only two children in a school of thirty that could speak a word of English. The country was one solid vineyard, the soil being peculiarly adapted to the cultivation of the vine. There were some two hundred children of school age in the district, but I found a strong feeling against educating their children in the public schools. The ministers of the two churches, one a Presbyterian and the other a Lutheran, both finely educated men, had large private schools where the children were taught in German. In fact, I was told that former teachers had failed to maintain a public school of more than a few scholars.

I started in with only ten pupils, including the two English-speaking ones. As soon as I could, I visited the Presbyterian minister, had dinner and spent the evening with him and his good wife. She could not speak a word of English, and he very little, though he could read and translate, and was busy translating a whole Sunday School library from English into German. I knew not a single word of German, yet we got on wonderfully well and became great friends. From this time on my school increased in number. It was surprising how soon an eight-year-old boy, without a word of English, learned to read and speak the language from a teacher that knew no word of German. I taught this school for three quarters, or nine months of school, putting in all my spare minutes and until midnight on chemistry, materia medica, anatomy, physiology, and other medical studies. I worked entirely too hard, and found myself broken in health and strength.

I consulted a good German physician, who, as near as I could understand, said "Resign your school, box up your medical books, and don't look at one for two years. Go home and rest for two months, and then engage in some other occupation. If you do not you will not last another year." I knew I must submit, and that once I had laid my studies aside for two years I would never resume them. So ended my hopes of a profession. I bade farewell to my many German friends, whom I had learned to like very much, and I think they liked me. The year I spent among them was the entering wedge that in a few years broke up the isolation of those good people and taught them to fraternize with the natives and in the end become good American citizens.

CHAPTER TEN

A BUSINESS VENTURE AND START FOR THE WEST

ON ARRIVING AT HOME with three hundred dollars which I had saved, I was content to remain idle for a short time, spending my days floating down the Meramec in my canoe or resting under the shade of the trees. But this could not last long, and soon I commenced to look around for something to do. From our home the nearest village was twenty miles. Scattered here and there was a country store. There was none nearer than seven or eight miles from our place, and I conceived the idea that I could establish myself in the business.

On our place was a landing on the Meramec River where the pine logs from the ridge were hauled and made into rafts and then floated down the river to where it enters the Mississippi, and from there they were towed up the river some twelve miles to St. Louis, there to be used for lumber piling, etc. I thought this would be a good location, so I immediately went to work with a carpenter, and by the end of July, I had a building twenty by forty feet, with shelving and counters complete. I had already gone to St. Louis to a firm who were engaged in the business of furnishing country stores, and as I was entirely ignorant of what I needed, they selected a stock invoicing about two thousand dollars, on which I paid my three hundred dollars, and the balance they carried for me.

In one of these stores were carried a little of everything, groceries, hardware, clothing, dry goods, patent medicines—of course, only in small quantities of each. Running a country store is not a very complicated business, and I soon learned and was successful from the start. That is, as successful as one can be in so small a business. I was my own clerk, janitor, bookkeeper and everything else. I had my breakfast home early of a morning and carried a lunch with me to the store, and at dark I would lock up and go home for my evening meal, then go back to the store, read an hour or so, pull a cot from under the counter, make it up, and sleep until morning with a gun by my side. As a good many rough characters visited the mountains, it was not considered safe to leave the store, a half mile from the nearest house, over night.

This continued through the summer and winter until March 2, 1858, on which date I was married to Miss Catherine

A BUSINESS VENTURE AND START FOR THE WEST

Patton, a young lady to whom I had been engaged for two years. Miss Patton was a well educated woman descended from two old Southern families, the Pattons and the Hydes, her mother having been a member of the latter family.

At the time of my marriage I was within four days of my twenty-second birthday by the figures, but looking backward and considering all of my experience, I feel as if I must have been ten years older, and I think I felt so at the time. It seems to me that I entered into the new relation with all the seriousness and consideration of an older man. At this time I took into a partnership a brother of my wife, a Mr. John Q. Patton, which partnership lasted until 1860, Mr. Patton staying at the store, while my wife and I resided with my parents, until I had completed a neat little four-room cottage close to the store, where we resided until the fall of 1859. During this year my young wife's health began to fail, and the doctor advised me to move to some more even climate. My brother-in-law had, in the meantime, married my oldest sister, and as he had lived for ten years in California, and my wife's only sister lived there, it was decided that we would close out our business, collect in our debts, buy the necessary horses, oxen and wagons and be ready to start across the plains early in the spring. Of course, we had to sell at a great sacrifice the little piece of land. My store building and cottage I had almost to give away. As we had to give up our cottage and sell the furniture, my wife and I went to board with her aunt who had raised her, her father and mother both having died when she was very young. I had to be away a good deal collecting together everything we would need for the long journey in the spring, but generally managed to get around once or twice in a week. On January 5, 1860, my oldest son, T. W. Hawkins, was born, and on March thirteenth we started on our long journey. My father and the balance of the family had caught the California fever during the winter, had sold the farm, and were ready to accompany us.

Our outfit consisted of father's two wagons and eight yoke of oxen, my wagon and five yoke of oxen, and John Patton with one wagon and four yoke of oxen—in all, four wagons, seventeen yoke of oxen, fourteen horses, some sixty head of loose cattle, and the party consisted of about twenty persons, including drivers. The wagons were loaded with all kinds of supplies likely to be needed on a six months' journey where nothing could be bought. Our supply included bacon, hams, salt, pepper, baking powder, tea, coffee, flour and a hundred other things which filled the body of the wagon to overflowing. We had also cooking utensils, pans for milk, and tin plates, tin cups, knives and forks. At that time canned goods were unknown and I have often thought how much better a trip of that kind would be now when one can have all kinds of canned fruits and vegetables, but when we have all these things and one could go pleasantly, who would want to go two thousand miles in an oxen wagon? Such is the irony of fate. The world surely "it do move" even if the sun does not. Of course, each of us carried a tent, but I do not remember that mine was set up more than half a dozen times on the whole journey. My wagon was so arranged that the load was covered by a floor on which we placed our bed, the wagon, of course, being canvas covered and the canvas could be drawn together at either end as much as desired, making the inside as private and comfortable as one could wish. My hired man pitched the tent for himself a few times, but it soon became monotonous and he fell into the habit of spreading his blankets under the wagon, or when it became warm, in any convenient place.

At the time we started there was no green feed, the intention being to reach the outfitting town of West Point and there purchase whatever we needed and strike out from civilization as soon as the grass was large enough to depend upon entirely. Consequently, we camped close to some farm every night, where we could buy fodder for our stock, and I was fortunate enough to get a bed for my wife and boy until we reached the state line.

Southwestern Missouri was even at that time fairly settled and we passed farmhouses every few miles. The country was rolling land, mostly prairie, after the first few days, plentifully watered with many streams, bordered by heavy timber.

Our route lead us through Rolla, then a village, now a flourishing city, Lebanon, Buffalo, Bolivar, Humansville, Osceola and Butler, to West Point, the fitting-out point for emigrants. Ten years before this time, I understood, there were hundreds of wagons gathered here, and thousands of men waiting for the grass to start. That was during the great emigration of 1849 and 50. But at the time we arrived there were only a few wagons and families waiting.

We met with no mishap of any importance until just before reaching Butler. We had to cross a creek with steep banks, and the road was cut down the side of the incline in a circular form. We had no water for ten or twelve miles and the oxen were very thirsty. I was ahead driving my own team and when the lead span neared the water they pulled the wheelers and the wagon so that the wheels on the farther side were out of the road and on the high bank. I took hold of the wagon as my wife and boy were inside, hoping to prevent it tipping over, but in vain I used all my strength. It came over on me, one of the bows striking me across the back and pinning me to the ground. The wagon came over so easily that my wife and boy were not the least injured, and even the load was not greatly displaced. As soon as possible the men from behind hurried up, and righting the wagon, carried me up onto the level ground, where a tent was hastily erected and a bed and bedding brought on which I was placed, conscious, but unable to move. Meantime one of the men was dispatched to Butler, on one of our best horses, for a doctor. When he arrived I saw a more than middle aged, roughly dressed man. He was an army doctor, had served through the Mexican War, and as we were traveling, living out of doors, and in every way like soldiers, he would treat me as he would a soldier.

The first thing he did was to open a vein in my arm, and I remember he had to use his lancet a number of times before he could get a drop of blood, and when it did start it was perfectly black, and so thick that it would hardly flow, but after it started, it bled more freely and I do not know how much he took from me, but enough to leave me very weak, and I found I could move myself a little. He then gave me what he called an army dose of calomel, a heaping teaspoonful, I thought enough to kill a dozen men, but he said it was a small quantity that was dangerous and would salivate. Anyway I never felt any ill-effects from it. The next morning I was better but not able to be moved. We lay here two or three days, by which time I was well enough to be placed on a bed in a wagon, and as it was not a desirable place to camp, a man was procured to drive my team, and we started again. Every time the wagon jolted I thought it would break me in two, but as it was only some twelve miles to West Point, I endured it.

CHAPTER ELEVEN

FIRST ACQUAINTANCE WITH INDIANS ON THE PLAINS

AT WEST POINT WE CAMPED on a beautiful, rich prairie near the town. Our tent was pitched and I was carried into it, where I remained for two weeks. I must have been quite seriously hurt, and for two or three years afterwards I could feel it every time I took a cold, but finally recovered entirely.

I had never driven an ox team in my life. We had each taken a man along to drive, while we rode horseback in the rear and kept the cattle together, but this proved an easy job, for after the first few days every cow and calf, when they saw the teams hitched up, would fall into line behind the last wagon and move along when the wagon moved and stop when the wagon stopped. The man I had engaged, I found after the first two days, knew nothing about driving, having been raised a blacksmith, and my wife wanted me with her, so I concluded to try driving, and though I was awkward and came near being killed, I persevered and (except for the ten or twelve miles while I was hurt) I drove every foot of the way, and walked practically from our home, the two thousand miles, to our destination.

We remained at West Point for two weeks and supplied ourselves with flour and replenished our stock along any lines that we found short, it being the last point where we could procure any supplies until the end of our journey.

It must have been nearly the first of May when we gathered in our stock, which had become in fine condition on the young grass, and started out away from civilization. I am not exact as to the date, as a little journal which I carried and in which I made some notes of our journey, has disappeared. Yet, as I follow up on our course, it is surprising to myself how much comes back to me that has been lying buried somewhere back in my memory.

Our route lay a little north of west, across a most beautiful and fertile country, which at that date had never been touched by the hand of labor and whose sod had never been turned by the plow, though in looking over the map today I see it is traversed by two railroads, and towns are so thick that there is hardly room on the map to place their names. Feed was very luxuriant and we made good progress. We ferried

FIRST ACQUAINTANCE WITH INDIANS ON THE PLAINS

over the Republican River and continued up the north bank, on a level road, and rich alluvial bottoms, mostly prairie, but on the river were the largest specimens of black walnut I had ever seen. We averaged a good twenty miles every day without fatigue to ourselves or to our animals. The first prominent landmark we met was Fort Riley, beautifully situated on the north side of the Republican River. We had not seen a house of any kind for so long that the buildings of the fort and officers' quarters appeared as palaces to our eyes. Leaving the fort on our left, we continued on up the river, passing the reservation and the agency of the Sacs and Fox Indians. We saw a great many Indians here, and they were fine, large, well-built men, and a little later on we passed the reservation of the Pottawattamies, the finest Indians I have ever met. Hardly a man of them was under six feet tall, and well proportioned. These Indians were remnants of some of the old Algonquin tribes. They formerly lived in the lower Peninsula of Michigan, but were later driven to Kansas, where they finally settled. From internal wars they were reduced to about four thousand, but had dwindled at this time to not more than one thousand souls. Later on those of them that were left were included in the Sacs and Fox reservations, where they still live.

Our route continued up the Republican River until we reached a point almost due south from Fort Kearney on the Platte River. Here we turned directly north and in two days camped on the Platte River, just below old Fort Kearney. The divide between the waters of the Republican and Platte Rivers consists of low hills, and the water and feed were none too abundant. We found a large number of Sioux Indians camped here. There were hundreds, if not thousands, of them. This acquaintance with these Indians was to continue for more than a thousand miles, and from all I saw of them a dirtier, more treacherous, thieving, lying people never existed. You never knew when you were safe, nor did they recognize any right but might. They would come into your camp as innocent as children, and then they had a faculty of picking up a knife, a cup, or anything, and carry it off concealed in their blankets. We soon "got on to them," and though we would follow them around watching every move, yet after they had said "by" and departed, we would be surprised if something were not missing. I still feel hard toward those Indians when I think of how many nights, weary with a day's travel, with others, I had to stand guard over our cattle and horses to prevent them from being stolen, and perhaps ourselves, with our women and children, being murdered. Our company was not a large one and from this time on one-half of us had to stand guard every night until twelve, then being relieved by the others. The next night we would reverse and those who had been on the first half would take the latter half of the night.

At Fort Kearney we struck into the old emigrant trail. The

principal outfitting place was Independence, Missouri, near where Kansas City now stands. This route was somewhat nearer than the one we took but we figured that by taking the less traveled route up the Republican and across the divide we would have less company and more feed. I think we were correct, for here at Fort Kearney we fell in with hundreds of emigrant trains, some with a great many wagons and large herds of cattle. We avoided those wherever possible and in the afternoon one of us would go ahead on horseback and select a good camping place where there was grass and water, and wherever we could find it a little way from the road. In this way we kept our stock in fair condition, though we never found the grass so fine as on the first part of our journey. For the next thousand miles there was but little or no timber and the emigrants depended entirely on dry "buffalo chips" for fuel. I must acknowledge that I had a most unreasonable antipathy against this fuel. It made a good fire for cooking, and really in the final analysis was nothing more than condensed grass. However, I do not remember we ever used those "chips" at my fire a single time. All the way up the Platte River there were creeks coming down to the river every fifty or a hundred miles, and sometimes hills on either side on which grew cedar or ash. At such a place I would select a dry tree as much as two of us could carry and sling it under the wagon with spare chains. Such a log would last, with care, for a week.

At Fort Kearney, we obtained from a trader, the first dried buffalo meat I had ever eaten. It is cut from the animal in thin slices and dried in the sun, without salt or any other flavoring. At first I thought it rather tasteless, but after chewing it long enough I found a rich, gamey flavor, which was delicious after living for weeks on salted meats. We expected after leaving Fort Kearney to soon be living on buffalo and antelope of our own killing, but in this we were disappointed, for we never even saw a buffalo, and while antelope were quite numerous, they were so wild that I believe we only succeeded in killing two on the whole journey.

Pulling out from Fort Kearney we continued up the south bank of the Platte. The first night, after a long day's journey, we reached the Plum Creek, where there was good, clear water and some wood. Wherever there was no creek running into the Platte we had to use water from the river and it was about half water and half sand. It had to be taken in a bucket and let stand for an hour before it was drinkable. I preferred milk. I forgot to say that we had several milk cows, and had all the milk we needed. What was left over was put in a jar in the back of the wagon and by night we had a nice plate of butter. The jolting of the wagon all day served the same purpose as a churn.

The third night out we reached Cottonwood Springs. Here some hills came down to the river and some fine springs bubbled up pure and fresh from near the center of a grove of cottonwoods. At the time we passed there was yet quite a grove of trees standing, though the stumps and half rotten logs told the tale of vandalism. It always seemed to me strange that a man passing through a country should love to destroy or even use more than was necessary when he knew that in the years to follow thousands of people would be passing and need the timber he was ruthlessly destroying.

On the next day we camped for the night at O'Fallons Bluffs, a well-known landmark where some hills slope down toward the river, ending in precipitous bluffs some hundred feet in height. They looked like mountains after the weeks of almost level plains, over which we had passed. Here, just below the bluffs and about fifteen miles above the junction of the North and South Platte River, the emigrant trail crosses the latter river. It is a treacherous stream with a sandy bottom, continually changing its channel and as there was no way to cross but by fording it, was very dangerous on account of the quicksand and changing bottom. The river is about one half mile wide, and of an average depth of two feet at this time of the year, but the water is so muddy that a man riding across horseback may be going along in water only to his horse's knees, when suddenly man and horse would disappear, and come up a little farther on, with the water only a foot or two deep. Under those conditions it was absolutely necessary that the wagons in which were stored all of our provisions should be kept out of those holes. On the next morning all of our livestock was rounded up and with every man on horseback, were rushed across without accident. Then we returned, yoked up the oxen, hitched on to the wagons, which were lined up close behind one another. With the women and children inside and two men ahead on horseback to keep us out of the quicksand, we started across. I decided to drive my own team, and as we had traveled so far, I thought I could cross and drive from the seat on the front of the wagon, but we had only proceeded a short distance when my team, as well as the others, seemed to become demoralized, and would pay no attention to the calls of the drivers, and in another minute we were all overboard in the water, using our long ox whips and some words which soon brought the team to their senses, but we did not try to ride again. Anyway, we were as wet as a mixture of water and sand could make us. However, with no mishaps and with nothing wet but ourselves, we reached the other bank and then drove about four miles, pitching our camp on the North Platte. This stream is much larger and deeper than the South Platte and the head waters came from the summit of the Rocky Mountains. Our road lay along or near its banks for the next five or six hundred miles.

CHAPTER TWELVE

OVER THE ROCKY MOUNTAINS TO THE GREAT SALT LAKE

From our first camp on this river, in every direction, the eye found only what appeared to be a dead level, except O'Fallon's Bluff, of which I have already spoken, and two immense towers of rock right up the river. They appeared to be about twenty miles distant, rising up from the perfectly level valley to a height of several hundred feet. The nearer one was called Court House Rock and stood up square from the plains. The rock foundation appeared to be of different colors and at this distance looked very much like an immense public building. The farther one was called Chimney Rock, and resembled an immense factory chimney, needing only a volume of smoke from its summit to complete the delusion. In the rarified atmosphere every detail was perfectly plain, yet we traveled up the river and camped five nights, or at least one hundred miles, before we neared the first, the Court House Rock. It was our habit, if we struck good feed and water, to unyoke our teams and turn the stock loose to feed, while we had our lunch and rested from twelve to two p.m. In this way we avoided travel in the heat of the day, and it gave an hour's needed sleep to the men who had stood guard the night before.

On the sixth day we found a nice place for our noon hour, exactly opposite the Court House Rock, which lay off the road apparently a mile or so on our left. Some of our young men took a hasty lunch, and telling us they were going to see if they could find a way to its summit, but would be back by two o'clock. We waited for their return until half past two, and, as we could see no sign of them, we who remained yoked up our teams, gathered in our loose stock and drove on about eight miles to where we expected to camp, thinking that as we traveled very slowly they would overtake us at almost any minute. As they did not appear we unyoked and turned our stock loose to graze, had our supper, rounded in the horses and cattle. The women and children retired and the few of us took up our positions on guard. By this time we were very anxious, not knowing what had befallen them, but not daring with our small force to send out a searching party before morning. About midnight we heard a distant call and answered it.

Pretty soon they came straggling in, hungry, foot-sore and

about exhausted. They said that on leaving camp they had walked over two hours, and nearly ten miles, and, as the rock then appeared as far off as when they started, they decided to return. It was already dark when they struck our old camp and found us gone and, after resting, they struck out on our trail, traveling slowly because of their fatigue and darkness and the difficulty in following our tracks.

On this broad plains not only was distance deceptive, but sound also. I do not know if it was the altitude, for we were pretty well up in the world by this time, or if it was that on the perfectly level plain there was nothing from which sound could rebound or echo, but it was a fact that a rifle shot sounded like a pop-gun and the wielders of our heavy, long-lashed bull whips, who in the earlier days of our long journey were proud to show off their prowess and see which could crack his the loudest, became discouraged and gave up their game. Speaking of those whips, they had a lash eighteen or twenty feet in length and a stock only four or five feet. A man who knew how to use them could make them crack like a pistol shot, or touch up a "leader" who was inclined to soldier at the full distance of both stock and lash. When I first tried to drive my team, I had a great desire to crack my whip as loud as the others. I never tried it but once. After watching them for a time, I was sure I had caught on, so giving my whip a mighty twirl through the air, I brought it back just as they did, but instead of the wonderful report I was expecting, the lash coiled itself a half dozen times around my neck. At first I felt sure it had taken my head off, but when I found it still on, I carefully unwound the lash and swore a mighty oath never, never to try again.

After leaving the Chimney Rock we continued up the North Platte, passing by Scotts Bluffs, a noted landmark of those days, and crossing the Laramie River near where it empties into the Platte. We camped for the noon hour a few miles from Old Fort Laramie. This fort at that time was one of the principal army posts in the West, and was garrisoned by a regiment under the command of a colonel. It was situated on some rising ground near the Laramie River and only a few miles from the North Platte. The buildings covered a considerable area, being built around a central square. It was almost in the center of the Indian tribes between civilization and the Rocky Mountain Range. I was informed that, although there was a full regiment supposed to be at the post, the force was often reduced to a single company, the other companies being out on scout duty. After lunch I rode into the fort, where I found soldiers on guard as in war time and I was halted and had to name my business before being admitted. I got from the commissary a few necessary supplies and from the post surgeon some medicine that we needed, and returning to camp drove on six miles and camped on some fine feed for the night. Here we were almost besieged by Indian women and children, begging or trying to sell moccasins or other work made from the tanned deer hide. There was an old crone who looked like she was a thousand years old, who had some really beautiful beaded work. I bought from her a little pair of moccasins for my boy, some five months old.

The next morning when we had been an hour on the march, and some twelve miles from the post, the colonel commanding, mounted on a magnificent war horse, with his wife as handsomely mounted, overtook us. He told me that the country for the next sixty miles was overrun with scattered hands of Indians and that he would have given us a guard for a few days, but that there were only a few soldiers in the fort and none he could spare. He urged us to make the best time we could for two or three days, to camp in the open, away from timber, and to keep a strong guard. It is needless to say we followed his orders and there was little sleep among the men of the party for the next two nights. However, we never saw even the sign of an Indian.

From Fort Laramie the road did not follow the river so closely, there being small streams of pure water every few miles, making their way from the mountains on our left. We were now approaching the great range known as the Rocky Mountains. The snow-clad peaks had been in view for some time and now, away to our left, almost in the center of the valley, stood out Laramie Peak, while as far as the eye could reach range on range and peak rising above peak appeared. Before us the low indentation into the great range showed where the great South Pass was situated, while farther to the North loomed up other and still higher mountains. When we were far enough along to be out of the Indian Range we continued slowly up the general course of the Platte, resting a week at a time on some beautiful stream with an abundance of grass. It was now the last week in June and at this high altitude the grass was at its best, and, as we knew that before us lay very many miles of barren land, we thought it best for man and beast to recruit here. About one hundred and fifty miles beyond Fort Laramie we again struck the North Platte, just below the mouth of the Sweetwater. Here the Platte is a deep, rapid-flowing stream, and as it came from melting snows it was as cold as ice water. At this point some parties had established a rude ferry, a small boat which was carried back and forth attached to a wire cable. We ferried our wagons at about ten dollars per wagon, but swam our horses and cattle without accident. From this point our course lay up the Sweetwater for about one hundred miles to the great South Pass. On the second day out at noon we camped at Independence Rock, it being the fourth day of July, 1860. Independence Rock was so named by some of the pioneers who encamped here in earlier days on the same date as we. This rock is an offshoot from the higher ranges away from the river and stands out almost perpendicular on its front, but I believe is easily scaled from the back. As there was fine feed and water here we decided to celebrate for the balance of the day, particularly as some of our nimrods saw a band of mountain sheep gazing down on us from a cliff high up on the range. They started out with high hopes of fresh meat for supper, but returned toward night, tired, not having seen a sheep. I was told that these sheep have wonderful organs of smell, can detect a man at a great distance and can only be secured by old hunters who understand their habits and how to take advantage of the wind currents. They have the most wonderful horns I have ever seen. Some that looked larger than the sheep itself, and they curl around in a manner that one would not believe without seeing. I was told that if closely pursued or cornered they would fearlessly throw themselves off a cliff, alighting on their horns unhurt. I do not know if this is so. In a long and somewhat observant life I have learned to take hunters' tales, as well as fishermen's with "many grains of salt."

About eight days' travel from this point brought us to the summit of the Rocky Mountains in the great South Pass. The ascent had been so gradual for nearly two thousand miles that I could not realize that we had reached an elevation of nearly fifteen thousand feet without any steep climbs. In fact the road up the Sweetwater was very good, crossing the stream many times, which was easily forded. Banks of snow still lay on either side of the road at no great distance, and the nights were quite cool. We camped at the spring on the summit, which is the head of the Sweetwater, and flows Eastward down that stream to the Platte, thence to the Missouri, thence to the Mississippi, and thence to the Gulf of Mexico, over four thousand miles. Only a hundred feet farther over there is another spring called Pacific Spring, the head of the Big Sandy, which flows west into the Green River, thence into the Colorado River, and finally into the Gulf of California, a distance of nearly two thousand miles. It is indeed the great backbone of the continent. The descent on the western slope of the Rocky Mountains is much steeper and more rugged than the ascent from the eastern side, while the soil is more rocky and vegetation less vigorous.

Our route continued down the Big Sandy to the point where it empties into Green River. Ferrying the latter stream we kept on a course up the Black Fork, over a rather mountainous country, passing near old Fort Bridger and following for a distance the line on which the Union Pacific Railroad was later built. The country looked poor and the feed the poorest we had yet met. Continuing we looked down from the head of Echo Canyon into a narrow valley two or three thousand feet below. To descend seemed almost impossible. The road was so steep that we had to lock the hind wheels of our wagons and then they would almost run over the teams. I was told that many cut a small tree and tied it behind their wagons, but we managed to get down without this. After the first few miles the road grows less steep and the bed of the canyon widens out to some extent. Here I noticed beside the road only a few feet from it, a new made grave and at the head a wooden board on which was painted "John —— shot for horse stealing 1860." The Mormons surely had a way to dispose of those who came in conflict with them. We continued down the canyon until we reached Weber River which we crossed, and turning abruptly to the left through Weber Canyon, we came to a small valley in the hills, and to the first houses we had seen in many months. We obtained permission to camp and turn our stock loose on some unfenced lands. As we had been living on bacon and salt meats, with no vegetables for so long, I sought out a large house which I thought gave promise of affluence. I knocked on the front door, but received no answer, so I went to the back of the house, where under a tree sat a large, solid-looking man with a babe on each knee, while a dozen other children, from two to eight years, were playing around. Two women were washing clothes in the same tub, while a third was hanging them (the clothes, not the women) out to dry. It was my first view of polygamy. The man, as all others I met later, looked fat and happy, while all the women looked tired and careworn.

When I made my wants known the man called the women, who came and each one took a baby from him, while he went with me. He said they had but a few vegetables, but finally produced a few potatoes and some onions, then going to the chicken yard he caught me two fine hens. Of course, I expected to pay an exorbitant price, and I was not disappointed. As we were not especially equipped for cooking chicken, we had a fine stew and added the potatoes, while the onions we took raw with a little salt. I don't think any dinner I ever ate tasted better.

The next day we continued through the low hills and shortly came out on an opening and the Great Salt Lake Valley and the City of the Saints was lying almost at our feet. The white buildings, the great temple stood out in the sunshine, relieved on every side by gardens and orchards and fields of waving grain. Even at this early date the Mormons had a fine system of irrigation and the city and its surroundings were like an oasis in the desert. At the city limits we were met by some of the city officials, who inquired who we were, where we came from and whither bound, and then we were taken in charge and piloted through the city and across the River Jordan on a substantial bridge and were shown a camping place on the banks of the river, while our stock was driven some four miles to the foot of some low hills, where there was an abundance of salt grass. It was poor feed, but they told us it was the best in several miles. The next day I walked through the city, which seemed well kept, a stream of mountain water running down either side of the streets. In the residence section the houses were large and generally long, with several front doors, I suppose to accommodate so many families. From ten wives up was about the usual number for the Mormons at this date. Brigham Young's house covered a large area and was surrounded by a high wall, and there was no admittance. I was told that he had anywhere from forty to sixty wives. Poor old man, what a time he must have had, and just think of the dresses and hats and all kinds of furbelows for so many women. Think of the shoes, socks, knickerbockers and little dresses for nearly a hundred children. No wonder the old man died, and no doubt he is reaping his reward. During the day many women visited our camp, with every kind of vegetable to sell or trade for a piece of bacon or a little flour. Anything of which we found we had more than enough to carry us through was gladly taken in exchange for vegetables, which seemed abundant, and very acceptable to us after being without so long. We also had some horse-shoeing done and replenished our stock with such things as we most needed.

CHAPTER THIRTEEN

DIFFICULTIES WITH INDIANS AND TRAILS OF THE DESERT

THE NEXT MORNING we recrossed the bridge over the Jordan, and crossing the city in a westerly direction, took the road around the northern side of Great Salt Lake. A few miles outside the city limits we passed some hot springs throwing steam up from their depths. A little further on we passed through a country of wheat and barley fields, which promised a bountiful harvest. At night we camped close to the foot of the mountains, from which some canyons came down, and where we drove our stock for food. We were about a week in making our way around the lake, which was almost constantly in view on our left. We must have passed through or near the sites of Weber, Ogden and Brigham cities. On reaching Bear River we ferried our wagons, swimming our horses and cattle in safety. Here we met with the only serious accident of our whole journey. We had recently joined another company from Illinois, as the Indians were reported bad, a little farther on, and it was considered also a good idea to present a strong front to the Mormons. The Mountain Meadow Massacre was of too recent date to be forgotten. Therefore, it was the custom for a number of companies to unite for one or two hundred miles through the Mormon country and that of their allies, the Indians. In crossing a river, it was the custom to mount our horses and rush the loose stock in and prevent them from turning back, and then cross with our saddle horses on the boat. In the Illinois company was a daredevil of a young man, and when the cattle were well into the river he followed them on his horse. He had about reached the middle, the horse swimming gallantly, when the man and horse suddenly disappeared. After a time the horse came to the surface further across, but we never saw the young man again. We camped on the bank and all hands turned out to search for the body. The ferryman assured us that it was entirely useless, that Bear River never gave up its dead. This was the only death in all the parties we were connected with during the entire journey. Satisfied that further search would be useless, the next morning we continued on our way, and during the day we crossed the Malad on a rude bridge. This small stream looks stagnant, but has a great depth. The water was said to

DIFFICULTIES WITH INDIANS AND TRAILS OF THE DESERT

be very poisonous and was of a green, sickly color. We were glad to leave it far behind.

Our road for the next week lead through the Goose Creek Mountains, the City of Rocks, and down into Thousand Springs Valley. This part of the way was very rough and hilly, with little feed and uncertain water, and the mountains were reported full of Indians. We had, at this time, joined in with a number of other companies, and had a force of about one hundred men and nearly a thousand head of cattle.

On about the fourth day out, in going down a very steep hill, the key came out of the bow on one of my wheel oxen. He was a big, wild fellow, and hard to catch. Our four wagons pulled out to one side of the road and all of our own force started in to capture him, while the balance of the train and all of the driven cattle, including our own, passed by. It was one of the longest day's drives on the whole trip, twenty-five miles to the next water. We were detained nearly three hours before we could start. The hills were full of Indians and we miles behind the main body of the train. However, we started on and made the best time we could over the miserable roads. We kept on until about nine o'clock that night. It was pitch dark, and we were not sure we were on the road. There was nothing to do but stop until daylight. We loosened the teams from the wagons and chained them to trees. If we had turned them loose as usual, they would have wandered off for water.

Without food for man or beast, not daring to start a fire, we put the women and children in the wagons and stood around with our guns until morning. It certainly was as miserable and anxious a night as I ever spent. As soon as it was light enough we started on and in about five miles came up with the camp on a stream of water with some feed. We turned our teams loose to drink their fill and to feast on the grass while we gathered wood and soon had our supper and breakfast all in one. We considered it a great breach not only of common decency, but of all discipline that they had not waited for us or at least sent back a company of the loose men to help guard our women and children.

As one of our company had been elected captain a few days before, we called a meeting that was pretty warm before it was over. A man named Webster and one Charlie Wingfield who had been with us all the way took our side of the controversy. After a time, seeing nothing could be arranged satisfactorily, and as we were about out of the Indian country, we told the balance of the company to go to, well, some warmer place, and separating our cattle from theirs, including those of the two that sided with us, we moved down the creek and lay over for a day, while they hitched up and pulled out. We never saw them again, though I heard that in the desert farther on, they had lost most of their cattle and a number of lives in trying some new cut-off on the road.

The next day we crossed into Thousand Springs Valley, and camped on some low hills. The valley is almost level, with hundreds, perhaps thousands, of springs bubbling up all over it. Some are small and others are as much as three feet in diameter and as the whole plain is covered with vegetation it is dangerous for stock, for if they should fall into one of the larger springs it would be impossible for them to get out. These springs, form the head waters of the Humboldt River down which stream we traveled from this point for nearly three hundred miles following in a general way the line of the present Central Pacific Railroad. Our course lay as near the river as possible, as there are but few tributaries, and we camped on the banks of the river every night.

In places the mountains come down to the stream, forming high bluffs. In such places the road would leave the river and wind through the rocky hills, in one place for at least twenty miles, it taking a full day over rough roads without water to reach the stream again. The feed all the way down the Humboldt was rather sparse and in some places nothing but sage brush. Yet our stock seemed to get on surprisingly well. Since then this has become a great stock country, cattle subsisting on the bunch grass and sage brush.

In about three weeks we had traveled the whole length of the Humboldt River, without incident, and pitched our camp at the sink of that river, where we found some good springs of water and hundreds of acres of grass standing two or three feet high, something like the California wild oats, just before ripening. Here we camped for a week, allowing our teams to recuperate on the fine grass and to prepare for crossing the forty mile desert marked on the old maps "Mirage Plains." Camped near us was a band of two hundred Digger Indians. Their Chief who called himself "Captain Jack" said he had lived a good many years at Stockton, California, and spoke English fairly well. He visited our camp and was very friendly until a young steer belonging to Mr. Webster was missed from our herd. Webster was a very excitable man and went direct to the Indian Camp and complained to Captain Jack that his band had stolen his steer. That afternoon the Captain appeared at our camp arrayed in his war paint, and with many oaths worthy of an Indian who had the whole California vocabulary at his command, said that Webster had lied about his people, and that he must have satisfaction. He threatened the old man's life and the lives of the whole party unless the offense was adjusted to his satisfaction. Things looked pretty blue for us, as there were only about fifteen men half armed in our party, with a large herd to guard beside our women and children. My brother-in-law, Patton, was the captain of the company, and he and I finally got the irate Indian to one side and told him that the old man was crazy, "heap loco." We had heard that the Indians have a great fear of, and even reverence, for insane people, and when we made him believe us, he went away, however unsatisfied. We then went after Webster pretty roughly and ordered him not to open his mouth again or go near the Indian camp. If he did we would surrender him to the Indians rather than to endanger the lives of our wives and children. However, fortune came to our rescue. That night a long horned steer gored a large and very valuable mare belonging to my father, so severely that we were compelled to shoot her. When the Indians heard of it the next morning, they came and asked for the dead animal, and when we gave her to them, they cut her in pieces and carried her away, body limbs and entrails, leaving nothing behind. After that they had a big feast and gave us no more trouble. I have no doubt they had Webster's steer also.

We now spent a day or two in cutting as much of the long grass as we could possibly tie and stow away in our wagons, filling our water barrels, and preparing food for the next day. At the end of the week, having made all the provision possible, we broke camp at daylight and started out on the desert. Our road led almost due south for the Carson River forty miles distant. A few miles out on the desert, we crossed a beautiful clear running stream of as nice looking water as I ever saw. We had been warned that this water was deadly poison, so rushed our teams and cattle across it without giving them a chance to take even a mouthful. I have often wondered since if it was poisonous, and if so what the poison was. At the time I supposed it was alkali but having seen so much alkali water since, I know it could not have been that, as it is never clear.

For the first ten miles the road was fairly good, then the sand commenced growing deeper and looser, making the traveling very slow. At the end of twenty miles, and about four o'clock p.m., we reached some wells of brackish water, which had been dug by some enterprising parties, and called the half way wells. Here we unyoked our cattle, bought some of the brackish water for them, and gave them the grass we had brought on our wagons—not a very large feed when divided among so many. When they had finished they lay down to rest while we had a hearty meal, though cold, except some coffee which we made over a few little sticks of wood we had picked up. About sundown we were all hitched up and started out on the hardest and most perilous part of our journey. The moon rose about eight o'clock and we had a clear night and no difficulty in keeping the road. The silence of the desert was intense, not a living thing within miles, save our own caravan, and we traveled on through the loneliness almost without sound. The hoofs of the horses and cattle and the wheels of the wagons moved through the sands silently as the night, nothing was heard, save the voices of the drivers and the impact of their long whips on the oxen as they urged them on.

Strive as we might, we could not advance more than two

miles an hour. And oh, the weariness of it! The wagons inches deep and the teams half way to their knees in the shifting sands, while we trudged along by their sides, slipping back more than half way at every step, yet compelled by voice and whip to keep every animal, all the time, up to the limit of his endurance.

On either side of the road we could see hundreds, perhaps thousands, of carcasses of dead cattle in the ghastly moonlight. The air of the desert is so dry that dead animals never decay, but dry up with hides, hair and horns intact, and so remain for years. Through the long hours of the weary night we struggled on. The moon was low down in the West. In the East dawn began to lighten up the horizon and just as the sun came up, when as it seemed neither man nor beast could have endured more, we came out on to the Carson River, not having lost an animal. Unyoking the cattle and allowing them to go down to the river to drink, we stretched ourselves under the wagons and in a minute we slept the sleep of exhaustion.

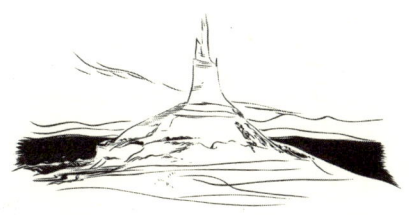

CHAPTER FOURTEEN

OVER THE SIERRA NEVADA MOUNTAINS INTO CALIFORNIA

WE STAYED OVER that day and the following night. The next day we took our course up the Carson River for Carson City, about one hundred miles distant. This is a country of sage brush and alkali, but the water in the Carson at this season of the year is fairly good, and among the sage brush there is some bunch grass on which our stock did very well.

On the fifth day we reached Carson City and camped near the town on some marshy land. Carson City was at that time quite a busy little town, it being just at the commencement of the great strikes of ore on the Comstock Ledge. By this time nearly all our supplies were used up, and, being offered a large price for the wagon that had been our home so long, I accepted and, selling such of our supplies as we would not need, put the balance of my things in one of my father's wagons that was nearly empty, turned over my ox team to help draw them over the Sierras, while my wife and myself concluded to go horseback over the mountains. The week or two in crossing was really the first rest I had enjoyed since we left Missouri. Every day, taking our boy with us, we would ride on ahead until we found good grass, where we would dismount and wait until the teams would overtake us, then in the afternoon we would ride ahead again and select a proper place for camp. When the teams came up we would put up our tent, as the nights were cold, cook a little supper and off to bed and sleep.

Anyone who has traveled in the Sierra Nevada Mountains knows how glorious and changing the scenery is. It was even more wonderful at that time, being almost a virgin forest. Our route from Carson City lay up a small stream, and, leaving Lake Tahoe on our right, we traversed three small valleys, then known as Faith, Hope and Charity. On, and ever upward, the road or trail wound around among the trees until about the third day we reached the summit and camped on the margin of the most beautiful little lake—a very gem—set in the summit of the mountains. As the banks and all around were clothed in a rich green and abundant grass, we rested here several days while horses and cattle luxuriated on the rich feed. We made a raft and went out on the lake, but could not get a bite. In fact, there did not seem to be any live thing in or on these clear waters.

After nearly a week's rest, we moved on. Sometimes the feed was very scarce. I remember one morning our cattle were scattered and out of sight. We started out in various directions to find them and it took until nearly noon to gather them in. The only adventure we had with grizzlies was on this occasion. My brother was passing through some heavy brush in a narrow trail, when looking ahead he saw a huge grizzly coming to meet him, but the bear did not seem to realize his nearness and came steadily on. My brother, finally, when they were within thirty feet of each other, gave a shout, and the bear stood suddenly upright, and the pair of them stared at each other for what seemed a long minute, when the bear turned deliberately around and took the back trail. It is needless to say that my brother imitated his example. He was not looking for grizzlies that morning.

The next place of importance we passed was the big trees in Calaveras County, known as the Calaveras Grove, where we rested for several hours and saw all the wonders of this grove to the best advantage, as up to that date fire and the lumberman's axe had not marred its grandeur. Only one tree had been felled near the hotel, and on the stump was erected a dancing pavilion twenty-five feet in diameter.

Our way now led down the steep Mokelumne Hill over a

very trying road. We crossed the headwaters of the Stanislaus at Murphy's, passed by Angels Camp, both at that time thriving mining towns. We were now out of the mountains and our horses and cattle, that had pastured wherever we pleased for some two thousand miles, could do so no longer, and from this time on we purchased the use of stubble-fields, wherever possible, and when we could not, we would buy a ton of hay. We crossed the San Joaquin River at French Camp, and from there followed almost the present line of the railroad through Livermore Valley and around the upper end of San Francisco Bay to Milpitas. All the way the plains were covered with Mexican cattle and everything was swept clean of feed, except in the enclosed fields. On our arrival at Milpitas, we learned that my wife's sister lived on a farm near Mountain View, only ten miles distant, so turning all my cattle loose with the herd and in care of my father and brother-in-law, who were bound for a stock ranch near Gilroy, I found a team and driver to take my wife and boy and our small personal belongings to our destination, while I followed, riding one horse and leading the other two. We arrived at the home of my wife's sister about noon on the thirteenth day of September, just six months exactly from the date of our departure from home.

So ended our journey across the plains. I have read somewhere the saying that the "Good Lord takes care of children and fools." Looking backward, I cannot but feel that we must have belonged to one or both of those divisions of humanity. We had started out on this great undertaking without any knowledge of its dangers and difficulties, without a guide or knowing what we would need most, and yet, we went on from day to day, not knowing what was ahead of us, and coming to our journey's end all in good health, having lost no member of our own party, and only one animal from our whole outfit.

When we consider that the best conducted and equipped parties expected to lose from one-third to one-half of their stock and often a number of their party on the road, it seems to me that a good Providence must have guarded our way.

CHAPTER FIFTEEN

FARMING IN CALIFORNIA IN THE EARLY SIXTIES

AFTER A REST of two weeks I began to grow restless, and to look around for something to do. I finally concluded, until something should turn up, to engage in farming. The fact that I did not know the least little thing about farming seemed to influence me very little. Perhaps the fact that I had been driving an ox team, cooking, washing dishes and doing many other things of which I knew nothing before, had led me to believe that one, if he just puts his mind to it, can do anything without previous experience.

I am not quite certain even to this day if I was not half right. I would not minimize the necessity of previous experience for the professions such as law, medicine, etc., but in the common walks of life I have seen some of the best farmers come from the cities, the best bankers come up from the janitor, even in engineering I have known some men near the top who did not have a scholastic education. I do not mean that any of these successful men would not have been better farmers, bankers, or engineers if they could have had an opportunity for a technical education, but I do mean that if one has the brains and perseverance he can overcome all obstacles.

I found between Mayfield and Mountain View a sixty-acre tract of farming land with a small house, into which we moved. With a little lumber I rigged up a kind of shed for my horses, and hay, and seed grain. The necessary expenses for a few pieces of furniture, for seed wheat, hay and barley for feed had exhausted every cent of the money I had on arrival, and it became necessary for me to put in the crop by myself. For my actual necessities, such as groceries, meats and vegetables, a merchant in Mountain View gave me all the credit I wished. It might not be amiss to say here that I have all my life been fortunate enough to possess abundant credit, and I count it among the greatest assets toward whatever success I have achieved. Credit is an absolute necessity, but must never be used to excess.

I procured a single plow and when the rains came in the fall I started plowing, and by the first of the year I had the sixty acres turned over and ready for the seed. As I could not risk my seed, I changed work with a neighbor, while he sowed for me. I watched his motions a little while and then asked him to let me try. He turned the sowing bag over to me and after watching a few minutes he said I had no use for him, and went home. I sowed and harrowed and in due season had my crop all in the ground. Then as it was yet early in the spring, I assisted a neighbor to summer fallow.

This year of 1861 was rather dry, but nevertheless, I harvested six hundred sacks of wheat, besides cutting some hay. The land titles around the bay region were so unsettled and there was so much litigation that I determined to follow the other members of my family, who had established themselves in the vicinity of Gilroy, in the southern portion of Santa Clara County. I decided on this more particularly as my wife's health, which seemed to have been re-established, began to fail, and I was anxious to get away from the harsh climate, which was more severe at that time than it is at present, since the orchards and other trees have grown up, breaking the force of the fierce winds that then swept up the bay.

Following up my intention early in the fall I took my family to my father's house and returned to sell my hay and settled up whatever I owed, and to straighten out the odds and ends that had accumulated during the year. In doing this I was detained until about the first of November, when taking what still remained of our household goods and my horses, I arrived in Gilroy. Here I rented a fine farm of two hundred acres of low bottom land, and started to repair the house so that we could move in at an early date. The repairs were never finished. My wife was taken seriously ill and continued to grow worse. We did everything possible for her comfort without avail, and on December eleventh, 1861, she passed away. Only those who have lost the companion of their young manhood can know the utter darkness that can come and the feeling that the bottom has dropped out of one's hopes and aspirations, that the world has come to an end, so far as one's own life is concerned. I realized, however, that hard work and unceasing work was the only panacea for me.

Leaving my boy, now nearly two years of age, with my parents, I moved into the old house without completing the repairs, intending to start on my farming at once. The winter of 1861 and 1862 was the stormiest I have ever passed through in California, and before I was ready for work the rains came in torrents day after day without cessation. The streams, swollen beyond all former knowledge, overflowed their banks, and the first think I knew my house was surrounded by water. I had left my horses in pasture, and there was no way out for me, except to wade, so I determined to stay by the house. Toward evening the water began to come through the floor and when darkness came on and I was endeavoring to strike a light, I found that the dampness had so saturated my matches that they would not burn. I used up a whole package in the futile endeavor. When I found it was useless, I felt around, put everything I could find on the tables, and taking my blankets, climbed on top of a pile of seed wheat which I had stored in a back room and resigned myself to pass the night alone and in darkness. But I soon found I was not alone. In the stillness I heard some animal climbing up the side of the sacks and I could hear it arrive on top and near my improvised bed, and then along over the bags. I recognized a pat, pat, pat, which I had heard before, and knew my visitor at once for a skunk. I suppose there is a prettier name for such a pretty little animal, but I don't know what it is. I have slept on the ground hundreds of times where horned toads, horned lizards and even rattlesnakes were likely to share my blankets, but none of those possessed the terror for me that this skunk did. I knew every hope centered in being perfectly still, so I lay motionless, not even daring to take a full breath. It is strange how easy it is to lie still when you don't have to do so, but how one's bones ache and every nerve tingles when it becomes a matter of necessity. My visitor seemed to be having a real good time. It would thump around over the sacks, over my feet, on my body or head, which I had taken the forethought to get under the blankets. All seemed to give him perfect satisfaction. How long he kept it up I do not know, but it seemed to me for many hours, and when I could hear him no more I was still afraid to move for fear he should be watching for me. Finally I took courage to turn over, but not to sleep, and I lay awake the balance of the night listening to the "rain on the roof" and awaiting the coming of the light. Taking it all in all, I think it was the longest and most miserable night I ever passed.

As soon as it was fairly light, I put on some old work clothes, and tying my suit in a bundle, I started for a neighbor's house a quarter of a mile distant.

Their house being on some rising ground, the flood had not reached it. The minute I stepped out of the door I was in water two feet deep, and in some low places it came nearly to my breast, and running like a mill race. At last I reached the house, changed into dry clothes, had a warm breakfast and was all right. The water was soon down, and on investigation I found that the fences in a dozen places and for a hundred yards in a place were washed entirely away, and down into a swamp a mile distant. As soon as it was possible for us to do so, we went down into the swamp, with infinite labor gathering the pickets, taking them back, and driving them again into their places; no sooner had we finished than the deluge came again, and washed away the same fence, and with it, more. This was repeated three times during the winter and it was not until March that I could get on the land with a plow. After my many misfortunes I only succeeded in seeding part of the land, and though it was so late, I had a fairly good crop, threshing about two thousand bags of wheat and barley.

When my crop was all in, I had rented a hay field of two hundred acres, and in May, I cut and stacked about two hundred tons of hay. I contracted it to a sawmill owner at a good price, set a hay press to work, and had teams ready to haul as fast as baled. The press had worked only a few hours when some way the stack took fire and burned, not only all the hay, but the press also. I lost, or thought I had lost in this fire, some two thousand dollars, and I had put everything I had in it. But later on I thought how true is that "There's a divinity that shapes our ends, Rough hew them as we will."

For the party to whom I had sold the hay failed a few weeks later and paid only five cents on the dollar. So if my hay had not burned, I would have lost not only the hay, but would have been out for the baling, the rope and the hauling beside. This summer, in particular, with my father, I had bought a header, and we cut and stacked considerable grain for others, beside our own.

I had, by this time, had a sufficiency of bottom lands, and for the coming season of 1862-3 I rented some upland north of Gilroy, put up a shack for myself and men, and a shed for the horses. My ill-luck seemed to follow me, and this season was very dry. In fact, the ground was wet enough to plow only for a few days. If I had stayed where I was, I would have hit it just right. All the luck I had was that the ground was so hard, I could not plow, and so saved my seed. Having had enough of renting, during this summer I purchased a farm of two hundred acres, four miles north of Gilroy, for two thousand dollars, built a house on it, and on December 9, 1863, I married Emma Day, a daughter of a neighboring farmer, C. M. Day, and early in the year we moved into our little house and started housekeeping. The summer of 1864 was even drier than the preceding year and no grain or hay grew in our vicinity. Having no crop to harvest, and hearing there was grain on the coast beyond Watsonville, I took our teams and headed over there and found employment for three months, earning enough to buy seed and feed for the coming year. I think it was the first heading outfit ever taken into the Pajaro Valley.

The winter of 1864-5 set in very early, with a tremendous storm of wind and rain. Almost all of the large barns in our vicinity were blown down, including the one on my place, exposing my little bunch of hay and seed grain to the elements. Luckily I had become alarmed and had made my way to the barn and loosened the horses and got them out just before it fell. I hastily improvised a slight cover from the debris and during the winter I seeded sixty acres to wheat, the balance went for hay.

During the next two seasons I farmed most of the two hundred acres, and all three years I had good crops. I had to haul the grain to San Jose, thirty miles, and I drove a team of five horses and two wagons, making the round trip in two days. It was pretty brisk work, and to load, drive the distance, unload and return, and take care of five horses took all of sixteen hours each day. In fact, these were strenuous years. In the spring, after the crop was in the ground, I would go to the redwoods, twelve miles distant, purchase from first hands a few thousand pickets, haul them home, and at off times sharpen them for driving. Then, after the crop was hauled to San Jose in the fall, we would distribute them where I intended to fence; then in the winter when it was too wet to plow, we would drive them and nail on a slat. In the three years in this way I had the whole place well fenced into four fields, at small expense. As proof that I did a good job, I went by the old place in an automobile a short time since, and those fences that I built forty years ago are standing apparently as good as ever.

In the meantime my family was increasing. In December, 1864, just one year after my marriage, our son Charles N. was born. In April, 1866, our son W. Irving, and in October, 1867, our daughter Kathryn followed. Having by this time increased my stock of farm horses, I needed more land. The place being in fine condition, I was offered six thousand dollars for it, just three times what I had paid. I accepted the offer, and in October, 1867, moved to San Felipe County, in what is now a part of San Benito County. This was then virgin soil. I rented a field of over one thousand acres, whatever I could seed, and arranged to put in two hundred or three hundred acres. The rains came early this fall, and we went to work with four single plows, and by the end of the year had all my seed in the ground. It looked so favorable that I took one team off and commenced bringing additional seed from Gilroy. The roads were so nearly impassable that it took four horses and two light spring-wagons to bring twenty bags, and the trip occupied a whole day. I kept pegging away, bringing in seed and sowing it until the second day of April, when we had in something over five hundred acres.

During the winter, while I was hauling seed from Gilroy, the road between Bells Station and Gilroy was infested by a band of desperadoes, who robbed stages and travelers almost every day, but fortunately I never chanced to meet them, or if I did, they passed without noticing a ragged farmer.

It was a favorable year, and I harvested over ten thousand centals of wheat, which I sold, delivered in San Francisco for two dollars per cental. At this time there was no railroad, so the grain had to be hauled by team to Alviso and taken thence by boat to the city. I found in San Jose a freighter with three big teams, fifteen or eighteen mules each, with a large and two trail wagons to each team. They could take from two hundred to three hundred bags of wheat to each team, and it took a week to make the round trip. With some additional help, however, they had it all in San Francisco a few days after I had finished harvesting. The freight to Alviso was forty cents, and from there down by boat ten cents per cental, so that the freight bill was five thousand dollars. With all the drawbacks it was a very profitable year's work.

CHAPTER SIXTEEN

SAN JUSTO HOMESTEAD ASSOCIATION AND THE TOWN OF HOLLISTER

IN THE FALL of this year (1868) I assisted in the formation of the San Justo Homestead Association, a corporation composed of fifty farmers, holding one share each. I was elected one of seven directors at the first meeting. We purchased from Colonel W. W. Hollister the western part of the San Justo Rancho, containing twenty-one thousand acres, for the sum of four hundred thousand dollars. Each of us paid in two thousand dollars, making the first payment of one hundred thousand dollars. We then divided the best part of the ranch into fifty homestead lots, being one for each member. We reserved in the center of the tract one hundred acres for a town site, laying the same off into blocks and lots. This one hundred acres is now in the center of the town of Hollister.

As all of the homestead lots were not of equal value, we decided to bid for first choice, and so on until we each had secured a lot. I had taken a fancy to the one-hundred-seventy-two-acre lot adjoining the town on the south. It was very rich alluvial land, beautifully situated, and it seemed to me that if ever the town amounted to anything it must grow in this direction. In October we held an auction and the first choice was awarded to me on a bid of four thousand five hundred dollars premium and of course I selected the lot that had suited my fancy. The next lot sold for a premium of four thousand dollars, and gradually grew less until the last man received his lot without any premium. The amount bid in premiums amounted to about one hundred thousand dollars, which, of course, went toward paying off the balance due on the purchase price.

At the close of the first year I was elected secretary and general manager of the association, which position I held until the debts were all paid and the corporation dissolved.

My position as secretary and manager brought me into intimate relations with Col. W. W. Hollister, a pioneer of the State, and one of the noblest men I ever knew. I can look back on my business relations with him with only emotions of pleasure. He came to California and, in conjunction with Thomas and Benjamin Flint, brought almost, if not the first, sheep ever driven across the continent. They became owners of the large Spanish grant known as the San Justo, which was afterward divided, Flint, Bixby & Co. taking the western portion and Col. Hollister the eastern, which we purchased from him. After the sale Col. Hollister moved his immense bands of sheep to Lompoc and Santa Barbara.

I was busy for the next two years in selling the town lots and the lands across the San Benito River, some twelve thousand acres. From the sale of these outside lands and the funds received from town lots, the indebtedness was decreased, so that by the payment of less than two thousand dollars every stockholder received a deed for his lot. About 1870 I purchased the one-hundred-seventy-seven-acre tract adjoining my original share on the east. This gave me a beautiful tract of land, about three hundred and forty-four acres, all of which at this writing is within the town limits and mostly covered with handsome residences, and some public buildings, among others the high school building and the Hazel Hawkins Memorial Hospital. The year 1870 was the last year of my farming operations. In September I had an auction sale, at which my work horses, wagons and farming utensils were sold to the highest bidder, realizing good prices and bringing in nearly seven thousand dollars.

In the fall of 1869, with the help of one man, I built a little five-room house on the site of my present residence, in which we resided for two years. In this house my son Winfield was born in 1871.

In 1870 the town was growing rapidly and I laid off the lands between San Benito and Monterey streets into one-acre building lots, which sold readily. In 1871 I sold a ten-acre tract to one J. M. Browne, who erected there a large general merchandise store and a flouring mill. Besides attending to selling my lots, I bought out one or two other farms, and during the year 1872 I also acted as manager for J. M. Browne in his general merchandise store.

This year (1872) I moved off the small house and built my present residence, into which we moved in October, and here we have resided ever since. In November of this year I had a severe attack of pneumonia and resigned my position in the mercantile establishment.

On the first of May, 1873, I started with a relative (Mr. Warren Patton) on a visit to my old home and the East. We visited first on the Meramec, but everything was so changed that I hardly recognized the old places, and most of the people I knew were gone. One cannot realize what a change thirteen years can make, not only in the people, but also in the physical aspects of a country. The Meramec and the country around about was a kind of battlefield all the years of the Civil War. One week it would be overrun by scouting parties from Price's army, who would carry off horses, cattle, hogs, corn, wheat, and in fact everything belonging to Unionists. They would no sooner be gone than a detachment of Union soldiers would raid over the same territory, carrying off not only everything belonging to those of Southern proclivities, but every man who was known to have talked too much was hurried off to prison or to work on fortifications. Of course, the reckless daredevils who took no sides would come through in bands and rob both. Every man able to bear arms was forced into one or the other of the armies. The consequence was that the houses and buildings generally went to rack. The fences were rotted down or used for camp fires, and the cleared fields had grown up with brush; even in the uncultivated parts where I remembered large tracts of open prairie there had grown such dense thickets of undergrowth that it was impossible to penetrate them. I do not know the cause of this. It might be a part of Nature's problem to turn the prairie in the fullness of time into forests, or it might be that the country was so stripped of horses and cattle that formerly pastured there that the wild growth sprang up unhindered. Although it was eight years since the close of the war, many families had not returned, and those who had come back seemed too much crushed to do anything toward the rehabilitation of their homes and fortunes. On the whole, I cannot say that my visit was pleasant. Too many vacant chairs at the fireside; too many desolate homes. Of those who had been the friends and companions of my young manhood, but few remained. Some were living elsewhere, but for the larger number, " Their graves were scattered far and wide, by mount and stream and sea."

After two weeks we took up our course and spent a week in St. Louis, a few days in Cincinnati, then two weeks of sightseeing in Washington, thence to Baltimore for a few days and a pleasant week in Philadelphia. From this city we went to New York, intending to spend two weeks, but after a few days the weather grew so warm and enervating that a great longing came over us for the glorious climate of our adopted State, so we shook the dust of New York from our feet and, passing through Albany and Buffalo, we arrived at Niagara Falls, where we stopped over for one day, and then on to Chicago for a short stay, and from there home. If I intended this for a book of travels, I could give many impressions that I received on a first visit East, but will only say that while it was a delightful and instructive journey, I was glad to get back to my beloved California.

One thought came to me very often. The Union and Pacific Railroads traversed a good deal of the country that I had passed over thirteen years before with an ox team. Many places I recognized, particularly on the Humboldt River, in Echo Canyon and on the Platte River. It was somewhat different in going over the same ground in four days at my ease in a Pullman car, to the six months of hardships and trials of my first journey.

But to return to my recollections. I must go back a few years. At the time we purchased the San Justo Rancho and laid off the town of Hollister, the whole country to the Santa Clara County line, and all to the south of us was a part of Monterey County, with the county seat at Monterey, fifty miles from Hollister and much more distant from the boundaries of the county.

Monterey was at that time a very quaint and interesting old town. The streets followed the natural contour of the land and wound around in a very bewildering manner. These streets were just as Nature left them, ungraded and ungraveled; in many places deep gulches had been washed by the winter rains. There were many very old adobe buildings. The principal hotel was a long two-story adobe, with walls some three feet in thickness and with a tile roof, as were all the principal buildings of the town. It had been the place of residence of many of the wealthy old dons that at one time dominated Alta California, and many of the old buildings were magnificent in their dimensions and furnishings. Colton Hall, a stone building situated on the hill overlooking the town, was historic, having been the meeting place of the Constitutional Convention, which convened here on the first day of September, 1849.

Around the town are many points of interest. In a ravine at the north end stood a cross, commemorating the landing of Father Junipero Serra on June 1, 1770. A little farther, on a commanding hill, stood the old earthworks of the fort commanding the entrance to Monterey Bay, with quite a number of the ancient cannons still in position. Many of those old guns could be seen in the streets of the town, where they had been carried and planted muzzle down at the corners of the streets. A few miles from the town were the ruins of the old Carmel Mission. This has been since restored and is an interesting landmark of the early days.

In my visits to this ancient town I became acquainted with many of the early American residents. Among those I remember best were Wm. R. Parker, S. F. Giel and H. W. Webb. Later on I made the acquaintance of Jesse D. Carr of Salinas, who afterwards became a stockholder and a director in the Bank of Hollister, and from this connection a friendship followed which lasted to the day of his death.

As our business increased and the sale of lands grew we found it a great waste of time and money to reach the county seat, where we had to go to examine titles and for all business in the courts. The Gabilan range of mountains cut us off from the rest of the county and seemed a natural boundary. In 1870 we began to agitate the formation of a new county, including all the territory east of the summit of the Gabilan Range. The

SAN JUSTO HOMESTEAD ASSOCIATION AND THE TOWN OF HOLLISTER

matter came before the Legislature in 1872 and, though we had labored hard for two years, the people of the remainder of the county, who were anxious to keep us, were too strong and our bill failed of passage. We did not give up the fight with this, but commenced at once doing politics, uniting all of the people on our side of the mountains, and by opposing everything the others wanted we hoped that they would in time be glad to let us go. I spent a good deal of time and considerable money in this fight. With Mr. N. C. Briggs I visited Salinas and the other towns, buttonholing the people. In the election of the fall of 1873, after a hard fight, we elected E. C. Tully to the Legislature, who was in favor of division, and after a struggle on February 12th, 1874, the Legislature set off the county of San Benito and appointed three commissioners, of whom I was one, with authority to call an election for county officers, and to set the proper machinery in motion, divide the territory of the new county into road and supervisorial districts and to perform such other duties as were necessary. Hollister was declared the county seat, and this was confirmed by an election later on.

On my return from the East in 1873, in connection with others, we incorporated the Bank of Hollister, purchased a lot and commenced our building, which was finished in September, 1874. I was elected its first president, which position I have held for nearly forty years, all the time being in active management of its affairs.

We have been very successful from the start. Beginning with a paid up capital of forty-five thousand dollars, we now have a paid up capital of two hundred and fifty thousand dollars, with a surplus and undivided profits of over three hundred thousand dollars. In the year 1892 we declared an extra dividend of fifty thousand dollars, with which we started the Savings and Loan Bank of San Benito County, which has also been successful, its capital and surplus at this time being in excess of one hundred and fifty thousand dollars, with deposits of over seven hundred and fifty thousand dollars. In all the years of their existence these banks have never failed to pay a dividend to the stockholders and have paid out in this way over one million dollars. At this writing the combined assets of the two institutions largely exceed one million two hundred and twenty-five thousand dollars. I can say that in the management of these banks our efforts have been not only to earn fair dividends for our stockholders, but also to use our credit and money in assisting our people in all honest efforts to build up their homes. I believe we have been no small factor in the great progress which the town and surrounding country has made in its development.

CHAPTER SEVENTEEN

BUSINESS INTERESTS AND ORGANIZATION OF CALIFORNIA BANKERS' ASSOCIATION

IN THE FOUR YEARS after opening the bank, I took an active part in other enterprises. At that time the county adjacent to Hollister was a great wheat and barley producing section. With others I bought the warehouses on the railroad right-of-way and built others, so that we owned at one time eight large warehouses, capable of storing twenty thousand tons of grain. This for a number of years was one of the best paying properties in the county. In fact, even yet they are good properties, but not to the extent that they were when wheat and barley were the principal crop.

In connection with Mr. N. C. Briggs, I also purchased the water works, formed a company and from year to year extended the mains and secured other supplies of water, until the town can boast of water in quantity and quality not excelled by any that I know.

Later on I was the largest stockholder in the company formed to furnish gas to the town. In fact, at one time I was president of the Bank of Hollister, Hollister Water Company, Hollister Warehouse Company and Hollister Gas Company, in addition to my private business.

Among other things I cherish is a fine gold headed cane presented me as late as 1892 by the superintendents of all the companies above named. I continued in all of these offices for many years, but during the last ten years I have been trying to concentrate my business and have from time to time disposed of my various holdings, until I am no longer connected with these properties.

In 1893 I purchased what is now known as the Los Vibors Ranch, two thousand acres of land, and engaged in stock raising. From time to time I have purchased additional lands adjoining until at the date of this writing (1912) I own some thing over six thousand acres, all well stocked, and the financial results have been very satisfactory.

In 1876, in company with my friend Mr. N. C. Briggs, I made an extended visit to the East, stopping over in all the principal cities and sight-seeing for a month at the Centennial World's Fair in Philadelphia. I enjoyed it very much, spending whole days in the art galleries and in the mechanical department, which particularly interested me. Again in 1886 I toured the East, this time being accompanied by my wife. Our travels took us through Cynthiana, Kentucky, where we stopped over for a week, visiting my grandfather's old farm and meeting quite a number of the friends of my school days. All the boys that were in school with me, and remained in Cynthiana, at the commencement of the Civil War enrolled in a company and joined Morgan's command and served throughout the war, and many of them fell on Southern battlefields. Others rose to distinction in the military and (after the war was over) in civil life. One of my schoolmates became a General in the Confederate Army, two rose to the rank of Colonel, while Captains and Lieutenants were everywhere. In civil life, one became a member of Congress, one was Governor of the Territory of Utah, one was a Judge in the Courts of Cincinnati, quite a number became bankers, while others attained eminence in the medical profession and at the bar. I do not think I have ever known or heard of so many men out of a class of one hundred who rose to some prominence in life. I do not know any particular reason for this, but they were the finest, manliest lot of boys I ever knew, with noble ambitions and high ideals of life. The environment in which we lived and were taught was the best, and perhaps it takes the "times that try men's souls" to bring out and develop all that is best in us. Perhaps among the young that I know today are many that need only some great occasion to develop noble men and women.

After leaving Cynthiana, we proceeded through the States of Kentucky, West Virginia and Virginia, visiting the Shenandoah Valley, the battlefields of Bull Bun and Manassas Junction and on to Washington City. A wonderful change had been made in the few years since my last visit. It was still the "City of Magnificent Distances," but new streets had been laid out, old depressions had been filled in and the streets were clean. I think it is the most delightful, as well as the most beautiful, city in the world. One can put in days visiting the museums and public buildings. In the Corcoran Art Gallery I found some of the finest works of art, both in painting and sculpture. Pennsylvania Avenue, with its broad sidewalks, its magnificent trees along either side and in the center of the street, has not its counterpart anywhere. After leaving Washington, we visited Philadelphia, New York, Chicago, and from there returned home, having had a most enjoyable vacation.

In March, 1891, I visited Los Angeles, where I met in convention quite a number of bankers from different parts of the State for the purpose of organizing the California Bankers' Association. At the close of this convention I was elected a member of the executive committee, which consisted of W. M. Eddy, of Santa Barbara; T. S. Hawkins, Hollister; A. D. Childress, Los Angeles; N. D. Rideout, Marysville; Lovell

White, San Francisco; C. E. Palmer, Oakland; W. W. Phillips, Fresno, and A. L. Seligman, San Francisco. At the first convention held in San Francisco, in October, 1891, all the members of the executive committee were re-elected and their terms of office extended to one year. Thomas Brown, cashier of the Bank of California, was elected president. At the meeting of the association in San Francisco in 1898, with M. J. Daniels of Riverside, E. P. Foster of Ventura, Frank Miller of Sacramento and J. E. Baker of Alameda, I was again elected a member of the executive committee for three years.

During the twenty-one years of my connection with the California Bankers Association I have missed attendance of only two sessions. During these years I have formed an acquaintance with a large number of bankers all over the State, among whom and their families I reckon many very dear friends. Hence these annual meetings have become to me a source of great pleasure.

In October, 1899, I was taken severely ill, a special train was engaged and I was taken to the McNutt Hospital in San Francisco, where an operation was performed for appendicitis by Dr. McNutt. I was in the hospital for nearly two months, arriving home on the day before Thanksgiving, very weak, but on the road to recovery.

CHAPTER EIGHTEEN

INCEPTION AND COMPLETION OF HAZEL HAWKINS MEMORIAL HOSPITAL

It was in the early spring of 1902 that I suffered the greatest sorrow of my life, in the death of my little grandchild, Hazel Hawkins, the daughter of my son, W.E., and his wife, Grace Hawkins. She had lived with us all her little life.

She was my constant companion, and we loved each other with a devotion I had never known before. All of her days she had striven unselfishly to make all around her happy, and when sickness laid its hand upon her, all that love and devotion and science could do for her was in vain.

On the fifth of March, as I stood by her bedside, she opened her eyes and looking at me said in her sweet voice, "Good-night, Grandpa," and then fell asleep, to waken in the Paradise of God.

No one but those who have lost their best beloved can know the utter loneliness and despair of such a parting. I cannot write about it after the lapse of so many years without my heart overflowing, and the tears will come unbidden to my eyes.

And so the years passed on, yet I could find no alleviation for my sorrow. On the second anniversary of her death, just as the sun was sinking to rest, I walked out to the cemetery and, sitting down by her little grave, I wrote the following lines:

> They told me when you went away
> That time would kindly soothe my grief,
> That fleeting days and passing years
> And changing scenes would bring relief.
>
> Yet twice since then the voice of Spring
> Has softly called the flowers to bloom,
> And twice have Summer roses shed
> O'er all the earth their rich perfume.
>
> And twice the Autumn days have come
> And turned to brown the distant hills,
> And twice the Winter's falling rain
> Has waked to life the brooks and rills.

Yet, as this eve I sit alone
And think o'er all the happy years
When you were here, my eyes grow dim,
I cannot see for falling tears.

And as I sadly think of you,
I wonder—wonder if you know
Through all these days with all my heart
That I have loved, still love you so.

That all the world is desolate,
My aching heart is empty yet,
And whatsoe'er may me betide,
I cannot, if I would, forget.

I had long been considering some suitable monument to her memory and about this time I decided that a hospital in remembrance would be what she would have chosen.

In the spring of 1906 I had the plans all completed and was preparing to start the work, when the earthquake of that year came and injured and destroyed many brick buildings, and the experience decided me to change the plans, and it was midsummer before the new design was complete and work commenced. The design shows an exterior of cream colored brick with trimmings of red terra cotta. The building is large enough to meet the demands of the city and surrounding country for many years to come. There are two operating rooms, and all the appliances that medical science can desire for the care of patients.

In November, 1907, the building was completed and with furnishings represents an expenditure of forty thousand dollars. Prior to this I had deeded the property to a board of seven trustees, consisting of N. C. Briggs, M.T. Dooling, R.P. Lathrop, A.D. Shaw, C.N. Hawkins, Wm. Palmtag and George H. Moore. On the twenty-third day of November the building was dedicated, and as I consider this the greatest work of my life, it seems to me proper that the proceedings should have a place here in full.

DEDICATED TO THE PEOPLE
HAZEL HAWKINS MEMORIAL HOSPITAL

Nature seemed to have reserved the fairest day of late Autumn with which to hallow the dedicatory services of Hazel Hawkins Memorial Hospital on Saturday. For a week previous it had been threatening rain, the skies were overcast, and the weather generally was disagreeable. But Saturday morning the sun rose bright and clear from behind old Santa Ana peak, the sky was blue and beautiful, the air gently stirring with Autumn zephyr and was balmy and delightful.

The hour of service was set for 2 o'clock, and long before that period an expectant throng had assembled on the grounds in front of the spacious building. People were there from all parts of the county to show their appreciation of the magnificent hospital just completed, and testify their esteem for the generous founder. The exercises were held on the portico of the main entrance. Seats had been provided on the ground for several hundred and many people additional stood during the ceremony, or sat in carriages clustered on every hand.

The exercises opened with a prayer by Rev. Wm. Goodpasture of the M.E. Church, South. A splendid choir had been drilled by Prof. John Dehof, who accompanied on the piano. The choir consisted of Misses Mabel Kearney, Sadie Hain, sopranos; Mesdames Chas. Wagner, E. Bolton, A.W. Cutts; Mrs. J.T. Lowe, Mrs. J.N. Dehof, Miss E. Garner, Miss A.J. Dehof, altos; Mr. H.C. Irons, Mr. J.J. Burnett, Dr. J.H. Tebbetts, Mr. J. Long, tenors; Mr. Thomas O'Donnell, Mr. Guy Hooton, bassos. The first selection was "Thine Eyes So Blue and Tender," by Schehlman. The music was beautifully rendered, each note sounding clearly in the open air.

Mr. T. S. Hawkins then presented the deed of trust for the hospital to Mr. N.C. Briggs, chairman of the Board of Trustees. Mr. Hawkins made a brief address. Mr. Hawkins' address was as follows:

"My Friends and Fellow Citizens:

"You must not be surprised, if in the few words I have to say today the personal pronoun shall frequently appear, for I propose to confine my remarks to my connection with the causes that have led up to the erection of this building, and to my hopes for its future, and leave to those more able than I, who are to follow, whatever more is to be said.

"I have much to be thankful for this day. I am thankful to my Heavenly Father that my life has been spared to see the completion of this, which I consider the great work of my life.

"I am thankful to see before me the faces of so many of my friends, whom I have known so long, and among whom I have lived for almost forty years.

"I am thankful to the noble physicians of this town, who have so greatly aided me by their advice and friendly counsel.

"I am thankful to the good women and good men, and benevolent orders of this county in furnishing so many rooms in such a handsome manner, and to all who have taken so lively an interest in this undertaking.

"We present to you this day a hospital up-to-date in every way. All that the latest knowledge in building, in heating, in lighting, all of the latest appliances known to medical science and the demands of modern surgery are here. To this place the sick and suffering may come, assured of every comfort and care, and here the physician will be surrounded with every appliance that will enable him to do his best work in healing the sick and ameliorating human suffering. No pains or thought or money has been spared to make it a perfect hospital. In this I do not arrogate to myself any credit in the performance. I have been but the humble instrument in the hands of Almighty God. If this building is beautiful in outline and proportion, satisfying to the eye in coloring, and in every way the 'house beautiful,' the credit is due to the architect whose mind evolved the plan and carried it out to completion. If it is built solidly from turret to foundation stone, to endure to be a blessing to generations yet unborn, which I believe it to be, the credit is due to the honest workmen who laid its foundations, built its walls and in a hundred ways wrought toward its consummation. I can not even claim the conception of this work. It is said in holy writ, 'And a little child shall lead them.' So from the beautiful and unselfish life of the little child whose name adorns these portals came the inspiration of all that has been done.

"For a few short years she was given us to be the joy and sunshine of our home. And all her little life she went about doing good—carrying the sunshine of her presence to little girls who were sick, helping the poor as far as she could. And in a thousand ways she spent her days in making others happy. And when in the wisdom of Divine Providence she was called home to dwell with the Savior she loved so well, I felt

I must, in some way, carry out the work she would have done. I could think of no better way than this home for the sick and suffering.

"And now I feel my life-work is accomplished, and yet I am not tired of life, and so long as it is His will that I shall linger among you I am content. I love this beautiful world in all its aspects. In Spring, when the flowers bloom and the air is laden with perfume, or in Summer with its fields of waving grain, or when Autumn comes and the distant hills put on their tawny robes, or when Winter rains come down with the promise of a resurrection and a new life, it is ever beautiful to me.

"Yet the fast flying years remind me that the sun of my life is sinking low towards the horizon's verge and the shadows behind grow longer day by day, and I can only stand and wait until the summons comes to call me home, when I trust that with the consciousness that I have not lived entirely in vain, and trusting in Him who rules the world, I shall go to my rest 'Like one who wraps the draperies of his couch About him, and lies down to pleasant dreams.'

"And now it becomes my duty, as well as my pleasure, to hand over to you, Mr. Briggs, as chairman of the Board of Trustees of Hazel Hawkins Memorial Hospital, this deed properly signed and sealed, conveying to you and your successors in office forever this building and the land surrounding it, in trust for the people of San Benito county.

"We give it to you as a sacred trust, to be used only for the purposes named in the deed of gift, and with the ardent faith that you gentlemen of the present board and your successors will see to it that these doors are never closed against those who need its assistance.

"Whatever may come, I shall trust that you will find some way to keep them open forever."

Mr. Briggs accepted the trust in well-chosen words. He said:

"Mr. T.S. Hawkins, on behalf of those whom you have named as trustees, I publicly accept this conveyance and the trust it confers. We fully appreciate the honor conferred upon us and the confidence reposed in us by you, and give to you the assurance that the trust you have confided to us will be executed faithfully and earnestly.

"We deem it not inappropriate at this time to extend to you on behalf of the people of this county, and particularly of the town of Hollister, their heartfelt thanks for this, your most generous gift to the public welfare.

"Traverse as you may throughout this Golden State of ours, you will not find a more beautiful city than Hollister. Above are skies as blue as those of Italy, and Nature's pictures surrounding it are as picturesque as those of far-famed Switzerland; and here, in the midst of this busy little city, the abode of a happy people, you have located this beautiful and substantial memorial gift—a building and location in every way worthy of the best thought and purest intention of any one. We have no doubt that you have given to its construction your best efforts. The perfection of detail in its construction, and its architectural beauty and surroundings speak forcibly of the anxious consideration given by you to the perfection of this means of relieving distress and perpetuating the memory of the little one who was most dear to you.

"In this community you have resided for almost a lifetime. You have done as much or more than any other in the building up of this city and county. In all enterprises tending to advance the welfare of your people, you have taken a leading part and borne your part of the burdens of life, and now this, the crowning effort of your life work, will be left by you as a monument of your good will to the people among whom you have lived so long.

"He who builds great monuments of industry, and gives employment to many people is to be commended; but he who relieves distress and suffering, and extends the hand of charity, without a thought or desire of recompense, is greater than all others. He who makes soft the pillow of pain and relieves a human being in his last efforts in the struggle of life not only does his part toward humanity in the journey of life, but adds a diadem to the crown he may wear in the life to come.

"We accept the trust and the work you have given us to do, and following the example which you will indicate to us in the management during your lifetime, will endeavor to continue it as a source of great good to the public, and as a monument to the pure and loving one whose name it bears."

The choir then rendered the "Slumber Song" by Loehr.

Judge M.T. Dooling then made the address of the day. In eloquence and choice of language the gentleman surpassed every former effort. He had a beautiful theme, and beautifully he handled it. The address stands our conspicuously as a tribute to the founders of the hospital and as a message to the people of the county. We give it in full:

"The occasion which brings us together here today, my friends, is one which should be of the utmost interest, as it is of the utmost importance, not only to every member of this community, but to every resident of the county as well. For today is opened and dedicated and given over to the public, and as we hope and fondly believe, to a long career of beneficent usefulness, this splendid Memorial Hospital—expressing at once the love of a great heart for an angelic child, and its boundless sympathy for the sufferings of mankind. And, indeed, it is a beautiful thought to dwell upon, that the passing of a little child, whose presence upon earth was as bright and as ephemeral as the sunbeam which she typified, should be the inspiration for a noble benefaction whose power for good is destined to continue through the long series of years that are yet to be. It is a beautiful idea as regards the living—thrice beautiful as regards the dead—that when you and I and all here present, who have borne a share in the struggle of life, shall have passed from view forever, this humane institution will be alleviating the miseries and ministering to the necessities of generations yet unborn—a lasting monument to the memory of a sunny spirit whose young life was a stranger to all the burdens and cares and worries of existence, but whose very presence brought sunshine into the hearts of her kindred, and through this Memorial Hospital will bring sunshine into the lives of many for an unknown period to come. One of the unseen evidences of immortality is the instinctive desire of the human heart to be remembered by those who are left behind. It is this desire which makes the soldier braver, the philanthropist more generous, the adventurer more daring, the wise more learned and the good more just. And this is a universal instinct,

> For who to dumb forgetfulness a prey
> This living conscious being e'er resigned,
> Left the warm precincts of the cheerful day,
> Nor cast one longing, lingering look behind!
> On some fond breast the parting soul relies,

Some pious drops the closing eye requires,
E'en from the tomb the voice of Nature cries,
E'en in our ashes live their wonted fires.

"And recognizing this universal and deep-seated instinct the philosophy and religion of every age and clime have conspired to rob of its terrors the gloomy atmosphere of the grave. The funeral pyres of remote antiquity, the lying in state of the royal dead, the sable catafalques of Christian temples, the last salute o'er the grave of the soldier, the silent prayers of sorrowing friends, the garlands, processions, emblems and inscriptions are but the solemn tributes all, by which the heart utters at once its undying regret for the life that is ended, and its immortal prophecy of the life begun. But no monument, no cenotaph, no emblem, no inscription, could supply a more enduring or impressive memorial to the dead—a greater or more lasting inspiration to the living—than this noble structure with its simple tablet which is dedicated here today. And we who are present, and we who participate, should not be content to dedicate this building alone to the high purposes for which it has been destined, but we should also resolve, in some measure at least, to dedicate ourselves and our own energies, to the carrying forward of the great work which is here inaugurated. For the thorough and complete success which should crown this work depends to some extent upon the assistance and good will of the community. Upon each of us at some time or another, must fall the physical ills of life and all of us should appreciate the inestimable blessing of having at our command an institution of this character provided with every modern appliance for the proper care and treatment of the helpless victims of disease and suffering. For no physician or no surgeon can do his best work except amid the conditions such as will surround his patients here. Conditions of cleanliness, of temperature, of ventilation, of isolation, of light, of every requirement in fine for which this building has been specially constructed in accordance with the most approved and modern ideas. All the great essentials of accessibility, of foundation, of structure, of dryness, of arrangement, of ventilation, of warming, of light, of furniture, of water, of disinfection, of everything which the highest medical authorities demand, and which are incapable of procurement in private homes, are here ready for the use of our people, and our highest duty, as well as our more selfish interest, demands that we co-operate with the generous founder of this institution in promoting its benevolent aims and lofty purposes. Here, too, will be a training school for nurses, whom modern science has decreed to be essential to the successful treatment of serious disease. And this is another matter of vital importance to the public, both here and elsewhere. For in the course of time those here trained and instructed in all the requirements of this humane art will be found wherever occasion demands their presence, bending tenderly over the couch of the afflicted, smoothing with gentle hand the pillow of wasting disease, lifting the helpless head of the languid and suffering, allaying the burning thirst of desiccating fever, banishing the grim spectres which affright the distempered imagination, diffusing a grateful coolness about the bed of dreaded pestilence, and encouraging with the well-founded hope of a glory beyond the grave those whom Heaven forbids them to restore in renovated health to a grateful family. And to these ends, with a blessing upon its generous donor, this Memorial Hospital is now formally dedicated, and given over, and launched upon its beneficent career—a fitting monument alike to the noble soul that is still on earth—to the gentle spirit that is already in Heaven."

The choir then sang "The Lonely Rose," by E. Hermes.

Dr. W.F. McNutt of San Francisco then made a brief address. He is an old-time friend of the Hawkins family. It was to his hospital that a special train carried Mr. Hawkins, some years ago, when life was hanging in the balance, and it was due to his skill and care that a precious life was saved for years of usefulness to this community.

"Mr. Chairman, President Hawkins, Ladies and Gentlemen, when I received the kind invitation from the secretary of the board of trustees, accompanied by the gracious and urgent letter of President Hawkins to be here with you today on this important and felicitous occasion, I could not deny myself the pleasure. It is a triple pleasure; first, that of visiting again this Eden of our glorious State, this garden of Eden from which I have never heard that your charming daughters of Eve have ever been responsible for the expulsion of a single man. Second, there is always a joy in meeting old and tried friends, and as we travel along the road of life we learn from experience to appreciate more and more the value of friendship, which is a rainbow of hope and promise when the clouds of adversity lower around our homes. Byron said that 'friendship is love without his wings'; perhaps it is love without his blinders. And, thirdly, Mr. Chairman, it would be difficult for me to find words to express the happiness it gives me to again take by the hand and to see the kindly face of my old friend, President Hawkins, looking so well, so young, and so joyous, and to find him engaged in this work of love, sympathy, tenderness and compassion; to find him turning aside from the struggles and toil in the accumulation of things material, to cultivate the things spiritual and benevolent and devoting his attention and his means to lessening the miseries, the pains and the sufferings of his fellow citizens. We are too apt to judge a man by what he believes, or thinks he believes, or says he believes; let us adopt that broader and safer humanitarian view which declares 'that they were judged every man according to their work.'

"The word hospital is suggestive of human sympathy and kindness. Hospes means host or hospitality. Now, your honored citizen, President Hawkins, is to be host to your sick and lame and destitute.

"And to entertain those less fortunate of your people and to extend to them his kindly sympathy and hospitality, he has erected this magnificent home. The sentiment, Mr. Chairman, does honor to the man; the hospital is an ornament to your city and will be a lasting blessing to those of your citizens who are overtaken by sickness and disease. Let us not forget that 'disease oft invades the chastest temperance and punishment the guiltless,' and that there are worthy poor and worthy sick. We will do well to ever bear in mind the words of one of the greatest poets and humanitarians of any age or country, Bobby Burns: 'Yet they wha fa' in fortune's strife, their fates ye may na censure, for still the important ends of life they equally may answer.'

"The hospital is no new invention of our day or our civilization. The Egyptian, the Hindu, the Greek and the Roman, had their hospitals. Egypt built hospitals for the treatment of her sick over 3000 years ago, and also had her college of physicians. Alexander the Great, long before our civilization, directed 'that the sick and wounded were to be carefully attended by the erection of medical houses or hospitals, and depots of medicines were established for the sick of both men and animals.' That the great religious teacher and humanitarian, Gautama Buddha, built asylums for 'the sick, for the destitute and the cripple.' His teachings and his sympathies had a broader foundation than ours. When he went out on his sacrificial mission he said: 'Therefore ride I not for man alone, but for all things that share our pain and have no hope or wit to ask for hope.' King Asoka established hospitals throughout his Indian Empire nearly 3000 years ago.

"The evolution of the hospital from what it was to what it is, has been slow. This was for no want of earnestness and devotion to their profession on the part of medical men, but the fault of their education—the lack of scientific knowledge. Until recent years the physician's education was philosophical and classical, rather than scientific. A knowledge of the classics and philosophy avails but little in the unraveling of the mysteries of the etiology and pathology of disease. It is to science and scientific research that Nature yields her secrets. The progress of scientific knowledge in the past few decades has been marvelous and no branch of science has made more rapid strides than that of medicine. And this vast amount of scientific work and research has been largely done by busy medical men, solely for the interest of truth, and for the love of ameliorating the miseries and suffering of their fellow creatures. The establishment of the modern hospital with its laboratories and scientific apparatus and with its staff of enthusiastic workers has in no small degree contributed to these grand and important results.

"There are always a few misguided, misled, illogical, but well meaning people, calling themselves humanitarians, who are forever making noisy objections to the scientific experimentation of our laboratory experimenters on living animals. The story of our hospital and laboratory devotees to scientific experimentation tells us that not a few human lives, as well as that of animals, have been contributed to that end, that the devastation of tuberculosis, yellow fever, plague, etc., may be stayed. The progress of human medicine and of the hygiene of infectious diseases which occur in man and animals are greatly indebted to laboratory experimentation on living organisms—in fact, it would have been impossible without it. The humanity that has for its object the prevention of epidemic diseases and the relief of pain, suffering and poor health to thousands of human beings of this and future generations is much more kindly than so-called humanity that would prevent pain or death to a few animals. Neither man nor animal can bestow greater love upon his fellows than to lay down his life for them.

"I cannot sit down without congratulating the people of this community in having in their midst a citizen who has conferred this great boon upon them—this beautiful hospital equipped with laboratories and every appliance that modern science provides for the treatment of disease. The modern hospital has become more than a place to treat the sick—it has become a temple of health. In the wards of the modern hospital, physicians and surgeons study the diseases and the treatment of the sick; in laboratories, they study the prevention of disease, which is often far more important to the community. Aye, more, the modern hospital has given us the training school for nurses. The trained nurse has become an essential part of the medical profession. She is a third hand and a third eye, as it were, to the physician and surgeon, and a ministering angel to the pain and anguish-tortured patient.

"From time immemorial, woman has always been our ready help in time of sickness. It is said that Helen of Troy administered to Ulysses and his comrades the 'sorrow-easing drug,' whose soothing virtues she learned from Polydamnia, the wife of Thone of Egypt.

"Our philosophy has its limits and our scientists recognize the handwriting on the wall: 'So far thou shalt go and no further.' The Providence which deals out mysteries that neither our philosophy nor our science can analyze or fathom sent his messenger of death to little Hazel Hawkins, ere the tender plant put forth its bud, and she joined 'that choir invisible, whose music is the gladness of the world,' and out of that sacrificial mystery rises this magnificent temple that is to restore to health and save the lives of hundreds of children yet unborn.

"We are here today to dedicate this hospital to the memory of Hazel Hawkins. It has already been consecrated to its benevolent purposes by her death and by the love and affection of a fond grandfather. It is only for us to leave here with the fixed resolution that we, too, will ever be mindful of those whose burden is too heavy for them to bear, and that we will not by thought, word or deed add one drop to the cup of the endless list of human ills that flesh is heir to.

"President Hawkins, when the place that now knows you shall know you no more forever, your name may be forgotten, that fell destroyer Time may erase it from the memory of mortals, but this monumental expression of your sympathy for your fellow citizens and your love for little Hazel Hawkins will be engraved with an iron pen on the 'Rock of Ages,' and the record of the deed will be immortal."

At the close of Dr. McNutt's address, the venerable Father Closa of San Juan, arrayed in the robes of the Church, gave the benediction. He read the prayer of blessing required by the Church of Rome, and enacted the solemn ceremony of blessing the building with holy water, and dedicating it to the service of mankind.

Then the grand building was thrown open for inspection, and from basement to attic it was thronged with people who in unmeasured terms expressed their appreciation. The hospital has heretofore been described. It only remains to say that visiting physicians consider it one of the most modern and complete in the State of California. It is a monument that will endure forever, and one to which every citizen of San Benito county will point with a thrill of pride.

In the hall is a bronze tablet inscribed:

"THIS BUILDING WAS ERECTED BY T. S. HAWKINS
IN MEMORY OF HIS BELOVED GRANDCHILD,
HAZEL HAWKINS.
1907."

In the years since, I have had no reason to regret my work. It has done much good in the community in ameliorating suffering. There is also a training school, where under the care of competent superintendents, a number of noble young women have been and are being trained for the profession of nursing. The Board of Trustees, at their first meeting made me manager for life. It has been a daily pleasure to me to visit, and by advice and in other ways, assist in its work.

Sometimes, we build better than we know. When the hospital had been running about one year, I was taken suddenly very ill, and carried there nearly unconscious. In a few days the surgeons opened the old wound in my side. I was confined to my bed for nearly two months. I am confident if the hospital had not been right at hand, with competent surgeons and nurses, I should not have recovered. I feel I owe my life not only at this time, but at two subsequent times, to the skill of the surgeons and the care of the superintendent and nurses. As long as life lasts, I shall never forget the faithful and loving kindness I have received at all times from everyone connected with the hospital.

My story is almost finished. It only remains for me to go back a few years and recount something of my more intimate family relations that did not seem to come naturally into the body of my narrative.

My father died in June 1890 in his eightieth year from the effects of a fall. My mother followed him in 1896 in her eighty-fifth year. We are a long lived family, and it seems to me a remarkable fact that of the seven children, who crossed the plains with my father and mother, fifty-three years ago, I, the oldest, being twenty-four, and my youngest brother, six years of age, all are still alive and in reasonably good health at this writing.

Of our children T.W. Hawkins was graduated from the Pacific Methodist College and has been for thirty years cashier of the Bank of Hollister. He has been married twice, his first wife, Miss Josephine Montgomery, bore him three children, Elizabeth, the eldest, married John Eggers, a mining engineer, who has been engaged in his profession both in Mexico and California. They have one child, John Eggers, who is my only great grand-child. My son's second daughter, Mabel, married Walter Little, a civil engineer, who is now employed on the new Los Angeles Water Works. Both of these young men are graduates of the University of California. His youngest daughter, Thelma, is a student in her third year at the high school. Several years after the death of his first wife, my son, T.W. Hawkins, married Miss Charlotte Roberts.

Our second son, Charles N. Hawkins was graduated from the University of the Pacific and afterwards he engaged in merchandise and later in the cattle business. He is at this time manager of the Granger's Union, a department store, the largest in the county. He is also manager and the largest owner in the Pacheco Cattle Company, president of the Moulton Irrigated Lands Company in Colusa County, and is connected with other enterprises. His wife was Miss Helen Boyns, a daughter of Richard Boyns, who a few years before came to California, from Penzance, England. Their children are, Pearl, the wife of Herbert Schulze, a merchant and land owner of Dixon, California, Thomas B. Hawkins, a student in his junior year at the University of California, and Charles R., a lively boy of ten years.

THE HAZEL HAWKINS MEMORIAL HOSPITAL

Our third son, W.I. Hawkins, after his graduation from the University of the Pacific, entered the firm of Eagleson and Company, of San Francisco, wholesale dealers in men's furnishing goods. Later on he took a partnership and the company was incorporated The Eagleson, Hawkins Company. After the death of the elder Eagleson, he became manager, which position he still holds. They have stores in San Francisco, Los Angeles and Sacramento. He is also interested in the Pacheco Cattle Company. He was married in 1891 to Hattie Latham, who died in 1893. In 1900 he was again married to Miss Edith Stark, and they have two children, Bradburn, eleven, and Elizabeth, eight years of age.

Our daughter Kathryn, chose music as a profession, and after several years' study in this State, completed her course by two years in Europe. She has been a successful teacher in San Francisco for many years. In 1890 she was married and has one child, a daughter, Marjory Boyns, now nineteen years of age. Our youngest son, W. E. Hawkins, died in 1908, having been for a number of years assistant cashier of the Bank of Hollister. He was married in 1890 to Miss Grace Dunshee of San Francisco. Of their two children, Hazel, "Little Sunshine" died in 1902. Their second daughter, Jean, is now eight years of age and with her mother has resided with us since her birth.

I made it a rule to spend freely for my children's education, and have given them some assistance in starting in life, yet have always allowed them to use their own reason in the choice of a profession or occupation. I think the success they have achieved proves the soundness of my judgment.

In conclusion, I will say that I have been a member of the M.E. Church, South, for sixty years, not that this particular branch of the church appealed to me above others, but circumstances have seemed to point to this church as my field of work. My religious views have been very catholic, and grow more so as I advance in years. I could have belonged to any other church just as well. Among Methodists, Presbyterians, Episcopalians, Cath-olics and all other denominations, I have found many good men and women, and number them among my friends. I have come to the conclusion that service and not profession is what our Heavenly Father demands of His children. It seems to me that the thousand silly dogmas that divide Christian people into so many denominations cannot be pleasing in His sight.

I have been a Sunday-school superintendent for more than forty years, and if I have been of any use in this capacity I have been more than repaid in having learned to love the children. My best friends have always been years and years younger than myself, and perhaps this has also served in a degree to keep my heart keenly sensitive to the feelings of others.

The larger part of the time I have been in good health, and able to do a good day's work in my profession. But the fleeting years admonish me that the time must soon come when these things will no longer interest me, and that I must lay aside the work and let the younger men take up the responsibility that I have carried for so many years. And as I stand now in the twilight of life and retrospect the past, I feel that I surely have been led by a kind Providence all my days in paths I have not known. I have much for which to be thankful.

There is no one in all the world toward whom I have an unkind thought, and I trust I have the good will of all mankind, and I have been blessed with some kind friends, whose faithful affection has made life worth living and very beautiful.

As I look out on the unknown before me I hope to go on during whatever days of life remain, doing the right as God gives me to see the right, unafraid and trusting implicitly in the love of my Heavenly Father and the hopes of an immortal life beyond. Until the end may I be able to repeat my favorite motto:

> I live for those who love me,
> For those who know me true;
> For the Heaven that smiles above me,
> And awaits my coming, too.

> For the wrongs that need resistance,
> For the right that needs assistance,
> For the glory in the distance,
> And the good that I can do.

SO HERE ENDS SOME RECOLLECTIONS OF A BUSY LIFE, BEING A SKETCH OF THE LIFE OF MR. T. S. HAWKINS, OF WHICH THREE HUNDRED COPIES HAVE BEEN PRIVATELY PUBLISHED FOR THE AUTHOR BY PAUL ELDER & COMPANY AT THEIR TOMOYE PRESS IN THE CITY OF SAN FRANCISCO, IN THE MONTH OF AUGUST, NINETEEN HUNDRED AND THIRTEEN.

GRATITUDE FOR THOSE WHO MADE THIS REISSUE POSSIBLE:

Thank you to the Hawkins family and its many tributaries: the Tuck family, the Meyer family, the Kingwell family, the Rogers family, the Eggers family, and to the many other families related to T.S. Hawkins, too many to name here.

Thank you Cressida Leyshon at the *New Yorker*, for her brilliant editing of the introductory essay. It was her enthusiasm and guidance that essay, and by extension this edition, into existence. And thank you to the *New Yorker*'s Neima Jahromi for his astute, relentless and exquisitely sensitive fact-checking.

Thank you Em-J Staples for her research, copy-editing, and for steering this book through all aspects of production. Thank you also to Claire Boyle, Zoe Kleinfled, Emily Clancy and Caitlin Degnon for their keen-eyed proofing. Thank you to Jordan Bass, Dan McKinley, Liz Hanley and Sunra Thompson, and everyone else at McSweeney's. Special thank you to Ruby Perez, McSweeney's staff member, born and raised in Hollister; her perspective was crucial to the making of this book and its new introduction.

Thank you to Jessica Hische for her customarily beautiful work on the cover and to Wesley Allsbrook for her elegant illustrations. Thank you to everyone at Publisher's Group West and Thomson-Shore for their support of this project.